Surrendering:

When Pain is Transformed into Extraordinary Blessings

Surrendering:
When Pain is Transformed into Extraordinary Blessings

KENIA NUÑEZ

BALBOA
PRESS

A DIVISION OF HAY HOUSE

Balboa Press books may be ordered through booksellers or by contacting:

Balboa Press
A Division of Hay House
1663 Liberty Drive
Bloomington, IN 47403
www.balboapress.com
1 (877) 407-4847

Printed in the United States of America.

ISBN: 978-1-4525-9649-5 (sc)
ISBN: 978-1-4525-9647-1 (hc)
ISBN: 978-1-4525-9648-8 (e)

Library of Congress Control Number: 2014907324

Balboa Press rev. date: 4/29/2014

For my children, Marken, Natalia, and Ava

Acknowledgments

A heartfelt thank-you to:

- ◎ God, for his incredible mercy.

- ◎ My Facebook friends: your likes, comments, and virtual love inspired me to continue writing through the pain, the joy, and the miracle of it all.

- ◎ My selfless mom, extraordinary sister, and fabulous extended family for their love and support in everything and anything I do.

- ◎ Pastor Dan and my Bridge Church family for teaching John-Marlon and me to trust in the Lord with all of our hearts.

- ◎ My community of amazing friends, old and new, who played their unique parts in our story—I am so blessed to have you in my life.

- ◎ Team Eagle, for inspiring me to crush my limited beliefs.

By his death, he gave me life.

As I watched his chest rise and fall, rise and fall, I knew the moment was coming. I wasn't afraid; I was grateful and humbled by a miracle akin to watching a newborn emerge into the world. I knew that when he took that final breath, he would breathe life into my soul. I had never been more certain of anything. And as I waited patiently to bear witness to this most miraculous transition from earth to heaven, I cried. I was overcome by a transformative peace, knowing that his purpose on earth was fulfilled in thirty-nine years.

When I was twenty-three years old, I recall my mom and my sister crying hard as they sat on my bed and watched me shove my entire wardrobe into black garbage bags as if I was a fugitive on the run. I was overly excited, not because I was leaving my chaotic home to live with my boyfriend, but because I was insanely in love and needed him like air; after less than two months of dating, we were living in delicious sin.

John-Marlon captured my heart initially by taking me on fabulous vacations and buying sprees. He bought us his-and-her wave runners and he bought me a car. He engulfed me with more love than I knew what to do with. I was in complete bliss, and I could no longer envision my life without this man. The gifts were great fun, but I was madly addicted to him. I had acquired the childlike wonderment that I went without as a kid, but I also took great pleasure in watching him live every moment as if it were his last.

As our relationship quickly approached the one-year mark, my feelings began to shift. I was so blinded by his tsunami of love that I failed to realize he was unwittingly becoming suffocated by what I thought was my codependency. Without notice, he broke free of the invisible chains that kept us interlocked physically and emotionally. In the process, he broke my heart. I was no longer his exclusive obsession.

I felt cheated. Although it was quite clear he loved me to no end, I was replaced ostensibly by random guy time, basketball, golf, fishing, paintballing, or just late-night drinks with anyone. His actions were becoming alarming because there was no rhyme or reason to his thinking. He was becoming a hard nut to crack. His obsessions and interests began to trump our relationship, and I felt more and more isolated in my own home. I didn't have a name for his behavior, but it was quite painful to believe that this issue was an issue he would have for life; this was not just a *typical man thing* that would come and go.

I loved that man more than anything, but I struggled with keeping up with his pace. He was a runaway train, and my entire marriage was about keeping up or being left behind. I now dreaded the very things I fell in love with—his passion, his impulsivity, his crazy spending, his generosity, and even his lack of communication. Yep, that's what I said—his lack of communication!

Our love and lust for one another ran so deep that it was all we apparently needed to sustain our relationship, I thought, but of course, I was insanely wrong. Not until three years into our relationship did I recognize that he lacked normal back-and-forth conversation, and it was a devastating blow because I realized for the first time how different he was. There was an uneasy feeling in my gut when I finally came to realize that all of our conversations were one-sided. They were all about his fixations, interests, and passions—never about my interests. I hadn't noticed sooner because I was willingly sucked into his vortex of euphoria—and that high was higher than anything I had ever experienced.

Life was grand, but it wasn't reality by any means! We were living in a wonderland. When real life came screaming out into the world at eight pounds, eleven ounces, reality slapped me hard in the face. Now with a baby in our lives, I realized I had two boys to raise.

In September 2000, I had a precious newborn, but I had also acquired postpartum depression. As I spiraled downward into my despair, my anger and rage grew. His insatiable appetite for more of everything and anything grew with my misery. He bought a boat, and then just a few months later, he decided to buy another boat when he discovered that the first one was too small to host his truckload of friends. We were a lower-middle-class family with two kids now, and I was not only embarrassed by his lack of judgment, but I had to start charging frantically on my credit cards to make up for the dysfunction in our family.

Once we had our third child, I began to suspect what was *wrong* with him. I considered divorcing him, as the thought of *fixing* him was too overwhelming; instead, I decided to keep quiet and deal with his erratic behaviors on a case-by-case basis.

In 2007, my son was officially diagnosed with Asperger's. I knew that I had to let John-Marlon know that he was on the spectrum too. Yep, I self-diagnosed my husband. I was fed up with living in a wild zoo, and I was about to drop the bomb that he was not as perfect and wonderful as he thought he was.

> Asperger's syndrome is a developmental disorder that affects a person's ability to socialize and communicate effectively with others. Children with Asperger's syndrome typically exhibit social awkwardness and an all-absorbing interest in specific topics.
>
> Doctors group Asperger's syndrome with other conditions that are called autistic spectrum disorders or pervasive developmental disorders. These disorders all involve problems with social

skills and communication. Asperger's syndrome is generally thought to be at the milder end of this spectrum. (Mayo Clinic)

In 2009, when I first approached him about seeking a diagnosis, he laughed and declined my "gracious" offer. However, after a few months of incessant nagging, I was able to get him to agree. He was then somewhat curious to see if what I had proposed was true.

He jokingly said, "I will get checked out for Asperger's—as long as you get checked out for crazy."

We both laughed, and I responded, "Sure, whatever you want."

Our laughter was short-lived, though. Weeks later, he walked into the evaluation a man filled with great pride and swelling with machismo, but he walked out with head bowed down, completely emasculated. The diagnosis and the process destroyed him.

After six hours of evaluation, all of his weaknesses were brought to light. Although I was not in the room for the actual evaluation, I held my ear to the closed door to grasp snippets of the exchange behind it. From what I heard, he couldn't repeat simple passages back to the evaluator, and he had serious trouble reading just a few sentences. I was devastated; I knew he had a learning disability that went undiagnosed as a child, but this evaluation was horrific. It was painful for him to become aware of what he otherwise had suppressed or was completely unaware of.

When I received the official written report a few weeks later, its conclusions were difficult for even me to believe. He was given a battery of tests, and instead of detailing the results of each of them, I will relate a brief overview of his neuropsychological status:

Conversational skills are restricted. In addition, John-Marlon is easily influenced by others into doing things at times when judgment should prevail. Reasonable changes in routine are not always tolerated. Sensory issues are also present. John is not always able to recognize and apologize for his own mistakes. He is not savvy enough to fully recognize and avoid dangerous individuals or situations. John-Marlon has difficulty coming up with the proper words to express his thoughts quickly. Academic skills are delayed in all areas.

Subject Area	Age Equivalent
Reading Fluency	9 years, 4 months
Understanding Directions	10 years, 1 month
Story Recall	9 years, 10 months
Communication	6 years, 9 months

I did not have the heart to share the report with him. How could I disclose, that on paper, he had the skills of a child in elementary school? I just couldn't.

So much of him began to make sense to me. He wasn't ignoring me; he just couldn't maintain meaningful communication. All this time, I had been trying to reason with a six-year-old trapped in a man's body. I was left speechless at these discoveries, yet the revelations drew me closer to my husband. I understood his unique way of being, and I had great compassion for how far he had come in life despite extraordinary obstacles.

He once owned three furniture stores at the same time. He was a successful businessman who paid off my debts several times over with barely the ability to read or write. I thought this was pretty miraculous, to say the least. He overcompensated by becoming self-employed, by his athleticism, his sarcasm, by being a man's man, by being a great lover, and most importantly, by engaging in a busy social life, which in hindsight meant he wasn't social by any means.

He was savvy enough to mask his weakness by pretending to be social. He would love to be around groups of people in loud places such nightclubs where there would hardly be any real communication. He would constantly host barbeques at our home—another situation where he didn't have to communicate. Instead, he would man the grill, serving people all day, pleasing them, making them smile, cracking awkward jokes, and when he had enough of the action, he would excuse himself to simply watch television in private. He showed brilliance by fitting into a world that he truly did not feel comfortable in.

When I did review some aspects of the report findings, he understood why he dropped out of school, why he had problems communicating, and why he lacked empathy. He was befallen by an avalanche of bittersweet information as he saw himself clearly for the first time in thirty-five years.

"I always thought everyone around me was an idiot. Now I know I'm the idiot," he responded.

My heart broke. I knew John-Marlon had a beautiful, brilliant, and creative mind, but I couldn't see how I would raise his spirits when I had just singlehandedly crushed him.

Post-diagnosis, I thought he would embrace the deficits and be willing to work on them to become a better husband, but that was so stupid of me. How could I ever expect this from him, knowing he was not wired to do so? And instead of helping him, I hurt him. It has taken a great deal to forgive myself for knowing that I did the best I could with the cards I had been dealt. The diagnosis literally destroyed him because he couldn't change into the person I wanted him to be. He now had a "fuck-it" attitude, and with that, I entered the most traumatic period of my life.

John-Marlon was dealing with great stress at work. The stock market crash of 2008 was finally catching up with the mom-and-pop shops. His overhead was $30,000, and every month, it was a struggle just to break even. He never expressed his great concern verbally; he only showed it through his terrible addictions and obsessions.

The strain of a failing business, plus the Asperger's diagnosis, had clearly taken him over the edge. I, too, was on the verge of losing my mind. John-Marlon was so careless and carefree about life that he would party two to three times a week with his so-called friends—anyone who would call him—just because he could. Heck, he had Asperger's and couldn't control himself. It became a little vicious cycle.

I would spend my nights on our bathroom floor, screaming, aching in pain for my husband to come back home. He would turn off his phone and never respond to my texts or calls. I felt like he despised me, and I hated myself. I felt I was the cause of the whole mess, even though I was smart enough to know that this outcome was not my fault.

Whenever he walked through the door in the wee hours of the morning, I would thank God and promise to be more patient. But I failed miserably. I couldn't accept John-Marlon's lack of respect for me. I couldn't accept him. In the midst of my pain, I would write emails—some to myself and some to him—because it was the next best thing I could do to losing my mind. I couldn't call him and curse him out because he knew better than to take my crazy calls.

I resented his Asperger's deeply. I hated him for keeping me a prisoner in my own country, in my own life, and in my own head. Yes, you read correctly: a prisoner in my own country. Let me help you understand by sharing the last sentence of his clinical diagnosis: *At a point, the Suazas may want to seek legal advice regarding a legal matter that occurred a number of years ago to determine if it were possible to have a more favorable outcome in light of new information.*

You see, when John-Marlon was seventeen years old, he got into legal trouble, and that trouble would affect his life and destroy my soul from the moment I decided to be his wife.

The crime: breaking a window with a screwdriver and leaving with a box.

The evidence: Two guys (one was John-Marlon) were picked up off the street, brought back by officers to the scene of the crime, and handcuffed in front of a police car while they waited to be identified by the witness. The elderly witness was then brought down to the building lobby to identify them from inside the lobby window, as "the assailants" remained handcuffed against a police car. She refused to go outside and take a closer look. She responded, "That's them." It was enough for an arrest.

After weeks of a hearing, John-Marlon was convicted of a felony as a minor.

Oh, how I dreaded putting this in print, but it is critical to my story to share for many, many reasons. When I married John-Marlon, I knew he had this felony conviction, and I accepted his truth that he did not commit this crime, but I did not truly understand the injustice that was done until I got hold of the transcripts. I had become obsessed with learning about Asperger's, and I began to understand how and why he ended up with a record. John-Marlon had the communication skills of a six-year-old—and he avoided confrontation in life just as he avoided them in our bedroom fights.

I could understand how he would agree to anything so that he could get out of it as fast as he could—whether he was guilty or not. It then became my life's mission to clear his name and rid us of both of the darkest secret that few knew—but had haunted us as if the world did.

As immigration laws rapidly changed since his conviction in 1991, so did the consequences for convicted felons who were not US citizens. Since John-Marlon was born in Colombia and never acquired US citizenship, he could be deportable just for breathing the wrong way. He was a legal resident of the United States, but none of that mattered with the new laws in place. Because of that, we lived every day like fugitives, except we smiled and looked like your all-American family. We literally lived a nightmare every waking moment, hoping that John-Marlon did not run a traffic light or have a social drink, get behind the wheel, and get stopped by the police.

Our three kids could lose their father should he be shipped off to Colombia, and for that very reason, it became my life's work to get his record expunged or cleared altogether. I was relentless in contacting attorney after attorney, and I spent my nights researching and highlighting his court transcript in preparation for this groundbreaking case I was bound to take straight to the Supreme Court—or so I thought. I was thinking big; it gave me comfort in my misery.

Every attorney we contacted agreed we had good reason to want to reopen the case, but all felt strongly that a twenty-year-old case would be very difficult to get in front of a judge. I was haunted by fear, but I used that fear to never accept "no" as an answer. When one attorney wasn't assertive enough, I found another attorney. I finally found one immigration attorney who felt strongly enough to consider our case.

The year was 2010. I held one of the most demanding jobs I'd ever had. At once, I managed a full-time job, raised three children, fought for the educational needs of my son with autism, dealt with John-Marlon's excessive behavior, and played lawyer—all of which led me into an abyss of depression and resentment toward everyone. I forgot how to be a wife, a mother, and a human being. More often than not, I forgot how to breathe.

John-Marlon continued to live his life freely as if he didn't have a care. He sometimes questioned my obsession with reopening his case, but at the same time, he had the wits to thank me for doing so—but not before spraying on Eternity cologne for yet another night on the town with the fellas.

I had it! I had lost my passion for living, and in anger, I would once again turn to my bathroom floor for that kind of comfort that only an illogical mind can find peace in. Sometimes I got creative in my despair and stood in front of my oval-shaped mirror to get face to face with the pathetic human being who stared back at me. I would cry the ugly cry and watch my mascara bleed down my cheeks, and all I could think of was how good it would feel to smash the mirror with my bare fists. I never did though; I was way too smart for that. If I injured my hand, I could potentially end up in a hospital. No one could ever know of my dirty little secret—that, at night, I would moonlight as a crazy asylum patient.

Below is an e-mail I wrote to myself on one of those very desperate nights. I would never send it to John-Marlon, but I needed to see my feelings on paper. I needed to be validated.

-----Original Message-----

From: Kenia

To: Kenia

Sent: Sat, Mar 6, 2010 10:39 pm

Subject: ok ... ...

You stupid motherfucker. Just got off the phone with you ... and this is how the conversation went:

10pm—

I am going out tonight for my birthday, you say. This is after going a week or so of not talking because you went out last Friday, and then because of your obsessive, compulsive robotic ways ... you decide that your fucking brain has to go out on Saturday too! You fucking freak. You don't even think it's important to include me in any of your plans. You give me a two-second notice that you want to go out, while I am at my mom's house, and you get upset because I don't have a sitter. You can't control the fact that your brain tells you, you have to do something! Years prior I thought it was because you were a dick, and didn't want me to control you ... but now I realize ... this is what you have to do to control yourself. You have no idea on how to stop your brain from doing something ... and you don't care to learn how to. So tonight ... you are going out as well! Three times in less than seven days. The kids haven't seen you because you have been working until nine o'clock every night because of the madness you have created by wanting to have fifty stores and not knowing how to run any of them! I can't even send this to you because if I respond the wrong way, you won't come home at all. It's not that I give a fuck about you coming home … but that I don't want you driving if you are going to drink, and so I have to eat shit, and allow you to come home, get dressed, and act like a fucking prisoner in my home because I can't tell you how I feel or your brain will go into overdrive, and you'll end up running away as you always do. I don't know what else to expect from our marriage. Ever since you have been diagnosed, you have plain old fucking lost it! It's almost as though you now know you are fucked up in your own head and so now there are no excuses as to why you are a dick. I am speechless! So the rules are when you get home, that I don't speak to you, don't give you a hard time, and sleep like I always do. I swear to God, I would never talk like this about my son, but dealing with an adult with Asperger's who does not want to be helped is suffocating, traumatizing, and exhausting. I WANT MY FUCKING LIFE BACK!!!!!!!!!!!!!!!! You don't fucking control me. You are playing on my weakness … so I keep my cool day in and day out. What man says he will leave his cell phone home and not come home until Monday if I fuck with him? I thought the diagnosis would be a blessing, but in reality, it has given you the right to be an outright asshole, and for me to prove to myself that I can eat more shit than I have had to my entire life. Once again, fuck you. I want my life back. It kills me to know that this will cost me my house, my life as I know it … but at the end, it will be okay to

*get rid of you. My goal was to help others dealing with
Asperger's save their marriages and create a better society
by teaching tolerance, but if I can't take the heat ... what
the fuck can I teach others? You are an evil robot.*

My eyes! I can't believe those are my words. It truly pains me
to read that, but I felt that this very awful e-mail needed to
be shared. I know that there are so many other women who
are secretly suffering in silence and think they are alone in
their thoughts, but you are more "normal" than you think.
We don't really mean everything we say in a moment of rage.
I, for one, know that is a fact. Our pain is a cry for help, for
validation, for love, or sometimes for a simple hug or a hint
of compassion. Reading this e-mail shakes me to the core. I
can't imagine those words coming out of my mouth today. I
am disgusted by the language of that woman, but I am also
so incredibly sad for her. This is what pain looks like when
it turns into rage. I was defeated and depleted—there was
nothing left of me.

One would think that we did not love each other as a couple,
but we truly, truly did. I take full responsibility that I did not
know how to be a wife at the time, but I also know that I did the
best job I could do. I, too, had my demons. I married a man with
an undiagnosed disability, who had practically raised himself, and
who lacked the communication skills that I so desperately craved
in a mate. We loved each other, but we didn't know how to love
each other. Still, in between the rainstorms, there was always a
rainbow, or at least a glimmer of one.

After trying to figure it out on our own, we began to see
a therapist. This did help somewhat, but I still found myself
trying to change a man who otherwise could not be changed.

We had this love/hate thing going, and I was exhausted. I was losing steam and began to tolerate his behavior, or at least I thought I was, until I encountered his latest and greatest obsession: the *Call of Duty* videogame. He would played the game excessively, and he would play into the night until the sun came up.

He would work until eight or nine o'clock every night and then race home to his new love. He was not only at war when playing the video game; he was at war outside of gaming hours. It was as if his nervous system went into shock; he had explosive moments and episodes of raging in situations that did not warrant the outbursts. I now had a defiant teenager on my hands. This behavior continued night after night after night, until one night when we had such a terrible fight that he threw the remote against the wall and promised me I would never have to complain about him playing videogames ever again. He meant every word.

Instead of playing *Call of Duty* until five, he was now leaving the house and partying until five, six, or seven o'clock in the morning. I had an afterthought about what an idiot I was. I literally pushed my husband out of our home! I should have just let him play his game! Once again, I hit the bathroom floor and did what I knew how to do best. What a disaster! What have I done?

My anger was dangerous at this point, and I did not trust my judgment anymore, but I kept my madness to vicious tongue lashings. I accused him of everything I could imagine. In my desperation, I started fighting dirty. I began to feed him lies that I was having an affair. Of course, it was not true, but I wanted a reaction. Nothing fazed him; nothing seemed to hurt him. Maybe if I told him I was having several affairs, but again, no reaction. When I realized that this idea was one big failure, I always ended by saying, "I just said that to piss you off."

I'm sure he thought I was even a bigger basket case than he thought I already was. On one of those nights, my rage was so intense that the agonizing pain I carried in my chest was too much to bear. I again let the venomous tongue loose without warning, but this time the rage literally caused me to black out. I couldn't remember what happened next. All I recall was him packing his bags and telling me he was going to rent an apartment somewhere, which was something he said he would never, ever do. He said he would never leave our children—no matter how bad things got between us. Something had triggered in him. What the hell happened? I wouldn't know that night, or many nights after; I would only discover the truth in those final months.

As he packed his bags, I begged him not to leave. Eventually, I think he was so terrified by my mental state that he agreed to stay—but with the agreement that we would just coexist in the same space. We were no longer a couple.

What else could I do but write another e-mail? I actually did send this one to him.

-----*Original Message*-----

From: Kenia

To: John-Marlon

Sent: Sun, Mar 6, 2011 1:41 am

Subject: The decision is made

Dear John-Marlon,

Who would have thought that you getting home at 7:00 a.m. and calling me to lay down next to you would make me feel like the happiest woman for that moment. You may not remember, but we were very intimate and I actually felt that we were connected like never before. This morning you got up and walked out like nothing ever happened. My heart felt crushed because I realized that it didn't mean anything to you. I died inside all day.

I am so defeated and sad and tired, and there is just nothing left of me. You have taken everything. I don't even have an ounce of laughter in me.

You gave me three rules in order for you to stay for another three months.

The first rule was that you are going away for your birthday. The second rule was that you can go out whenever you want, however long you want, but you will always leave the car. I cannot even remember what the third rule is anymore, but the point is that you are breaking the very rules you created. In other words, nothing matters to you anymore.

You told me tonight you were going to be with George and when I saw him on Facebook and then call you to ask you why you lied, you refused to answer. Why are you humiliating me in this process?

John-Marlon, the bottom line is that you have checked out, and I am trying to hold on, and there is nothing to hold on to. When your husband gets home from hanging out at 7:00 am, gets sexual with you, ignores you the next day, and lies to you about who he is hanging out with, refuses to take your calls, what can possibly be different from living here and living in your own apartment?

I am ready to let you go. You being here is too painful, and stupid me just realized that I am not a ragdoll to stand by for three months as my husband takes me for the biggest fool. The rejection, the mental games, is unbearable.

This is going to be the most difficult time of my life, but I am ready now. Now I know there is no Marlon and Kenia, there is no family. You made it clear you are not in love with me, and although hard to accept, I am letting you go because I care for the well-being of our children.

I don't know what else to say, except that I am sorry for any pain I have caused you. I hope one day you too can apologize for the knife you stuck in my heart and twisted with no compassion as you watched me fall apart.

I could not help you with your Asperger's, but you should never forget you have it so that you can make an effort to refine some things about you that have caused you to have communication problems with people. Please stay away from any trouble for our

children's sake. We have to protect them and put our
selfishness aside. Please! That I beg you.

Kenia

I had lost the war and given up. I didn't even have the energy
to kick him out anymore. Ironically, I never prayed to God for
anything. I just cried to him when I was desperate. Even through
the worst period of my life, I lacked faith. Not because I didn't
have it—but because I didn't realize how attainable it was. I had
no idea I could have made special requests to God. How did I
not know this?

An intervention by God eventually took place. I can't even
take credit for praying because I truly did not even know to pray
for healing our hearts. I was too broken to make any sense of the
life I was leading—until a miracle happened.

In March 2011, a friend posted on Facebook that she was
giving away a complimentary two-night stay at a New Orleans
luxury hotel. The moment I saw that post, I knew this was the
way to win my husband over—a forced vacation! Heck, I didn't
plan it; it just fell into my lap. Although John-Marlon and I
were not on speaking terms, I mustered the courage to ask
him to join me on this trip as a "friend," not as "my husband."
When I posed this question to him, he looked past me as if I
didn't even exist. I found myself having to think quick, and
all I could do was drop to my knees and beg him to come with
me. I was so desperate for him to love me again I begged to no
end from way deep, deep in my soul and cried frantically for
him to take note of my desperation. I wanted just one more
chance, and all I got was that look on his face—that look of
disgust. He responded with a simple no and told me to get off

my knees. He then just walked away, leaving me there with my hands clasped and feeling like a helpless fool. But although I lost hope, God sure had not.

God is good! Just a few days after my New Orleans begathon, John-Marlon began to drop subtle hints that he wasn't giving up just yet. I don't recall what the exact signs were from him, but they prompted me to write this e-mail to him. This one I not only sent, but I received a response as well. Can we get a woo-hoo?

------Original Message------

From: Kenia

To: Marlon Suaza

Subject: Saw you called me last night

Sent: Apr 13, 2011 8:41 AM

Good morning. Thanks for talking to me yesterday.

You have always told me that I didn't know you. You were right, but please understand ... you can't say that anymore. In all my sadness, I am very aware of who you are now.

Lesson #1

You showed your love through food and paying attention to things I may want. I NOW KNOW. You don't need to say "I love you" for me to know you love me.

Lesson #2

> *An argument cannot last more than five minutes. I NOW KNOW that after five minutes you shut down. I thought I could go on forever since you never reacted. I am so sorry I didn't know you need space when things get heated. My college education did not prepare me for love. I am learning.*

Lesson #3

> *Rejecting you sexually and saying nasty, horrible things to get your attention is the worst thing I could have ever done. I NOW know that you are a literal thinker, and I am not. I can't say things I don't mean, because you will believe them. Again, if I would have stuck to the five-min-argument rule, I would have never been in this ugly mess.*

> *You are not my son. You are my fun, sarcastic, green-eyed cutie that I fell so hard and fast for.*

> *I love you just the way you are and don't need you to change. All I need you to do is give me a chance to show you that I finally know you and respect you. I took your actions to mean that you didn't care, when all along you did. I am learning about me too in this process.*

> *You are a beautiful father, and I thank you and I love you.*

His response:

john <john@funsofa.com> wrote:

I read it thank you

From April through September 2011, our relationship entered the healing zone. We were not lustfully in love as we had been during our dating years; we were respectfully in love. We had a newfound perception of what we had been through and where we were headed. Ironically, neither one of us brought up the awful months when we had failed each other. It was forgiveness that did not have to be expressed—our eyes said it all. We took a few vacations as a family, but we also escaped as a couple. We made out like secret lovers, texted each other like teenagers, and actually began to communicate effectively for the first time in our eleven years of marriage. I thought this was the beginning of forever. I had my husband back, and this time I was loving him without conditions. I was ready to accept every little part of him, just as he always accepted me for who I was. Thank you, God, for giving us another opportunity to make this right.

One mid-October evening, our life changed forever. John-Marlon came home early from basketball and claimed he was not feeling well. He looked completely fine, and I thought he was too proud to say he wanted to come home and spend time with me. We were crazy in love, and our bedroom was seeing a lot of action lately. I thought he couldn't resist me, but then logic set in. He had never missed a basketball game unless he was injured or suffered a broken bone—and I immediately believed he didn't feel well. That day of not feeling so well led to weeks of alarming symptoms that included an awful dry cough, weight loss, a fever, and night sweats every night. After three months of testing, we were now faced with the most damning time in our lives: stage II cancer was now residing in our home.

And just like that, in eighteen months, cancer would claim my husband. He passed on May 7, 2013.

This book is a tribute to our love story and the invaluable lessons we learned in the face of tragedy. I am at peace in knowing that my husband's purpose on this earth was fulfilled; he was only meant to live thirty-nine years. I am now fulfilling my purpose as I immerse myself as a purposeful storyteller, leaving an impression on those who are meant to receive it. My hope is that you are that person.

(Facebook posts and journal entries are from May through December 2013.)

5.7.13

I want to thank everyone for the heartfelt support I have received with the passing of my husband. My heart breaks to know I will never see him again on this earth, but it rejoices in knowing that it is not forever. I am also comforted by reading all of your messages, literally showering me with strength and energy. I am eternally grateful and humbled. He fought an amazing fight, and he left no stone unturned when it came to finding a cure. I am proud of our teamwork!

His children were so important to him that I'm sure he timed his passing perfectly so that I can attend the girls' dance recital pictures today. So, at 11:22 a.m., he took his last breath with me holding his hand. He was at peace because he lived an amazing life. As I left the hospital, I was presented with the most beautiful clear blue sky, reminding me that life must go on. Till we meet again, John-Marlon!

5.8.13

I miss you so much, John-Marlon, though I am at peace knowing that you are no longer suffering. I am overjoyed you chose me as your wife. I am blessed you gave me three beautiful children, each reminding me of you in their own ways. I wouldn't change our journey, as it was God's plan for us, but I can't help but want to feel your touch again, see your smile, and see those sparkling green eyes! May you rest in peace. I will forever love you. Thank you for fighting the fight like no other. Thank you for letting go when you knew it was time. Thank you for letting me hold your hand as you took your last breath. I smiled when you left this earth because I knew you were in the presence of Jesus. I will live with purpose, just as you did in your thirty-nine short, but blessed, years.

5.9.13 (Day of His Funeral)

The thought that entered my mind as I prepared to pay final respects to my husband was how he never complained. John-Marlon was three months into having cancer, and he was still taking our kids snowboarding and skiing, and he continued to do so throughout. He never complained. Well, he did, but only when others didn't want to live life as fully as he did. When the doctor thought he had just two weeks to live, he went to Florida with his buddies, and he outlived what they thought by months. I am the luckiest woman in the world to have shared fifteen years with someone so pure. Today, when sadness overcomes me, I will do my absolute best to remember our rich lives together. We wear white to celebrate his life, and not to mourn his death.

5.11.13

We watched Phillip Phillips win *American Idol* together, and although he wasn't John-Marlon's favorite throughout the competition, he ended up being his favorite in the end. Yesterday, as we celebrated, we played "Gone, Gone, Gone," and videos of our lives flashed like a movie on a big screen.

I cannot imagine a more perfect song to represent my relationship with my husband in his final months, and my long-distance relationship with him now. Phillips might as well have written this song for us! Listen to the song. Read the lyrics to make your heart soar. Appreciate and love those around you. Spend time with those who matter. When it is all said and done, there are no do-overs. This will remain one of my favorite songs of all time. Thank you again for the amazing support.

5. 12.13 (Mother's Day)

Tuesday, May 7, was one of the saddest days of my life. Just five days later, I am now faced with Mother's Day. I will rejoice in your honor. I miss you so much! I know today we would have had a BBQ, but I'm opting not to take over that tradition just yet. :) At this moment, this morning, I am managing well, but you already know that. Please continue to keep me strong because in a matter of weeks we have Ava's kindergarten graduation, her birthday, recitals, and Father's Day coming up. Keep us strong please.

To my Facebook family, many of you have asked how the kids are doing. At this moment, they are watching *America's Funniest Home Videos*, and they are happy today. Every day will be different, I'm sure. I continue to remind them how blessed they are, and that their dad was unique. Not all dads are as amazing, adventurous, or as loving as John-Marlon was. He captured more memories with his children in his short life than most fathers would create in a lifetime. He was special. God is good.

5.13.13

I woke up a few times last night wondering if my life was indeed what it is. It only took a second to realize that "Yes, it's true ... he is gone." I went back to sleep like a baby both times. I read *Footprints* to John-Marlon the night before he passed, and he smiled so big and nodded in total agreement. Today, I also woke up smiling because I know that God is doing the same for me during this difficult time.

In the last couple of days, people have "secretly" asked others if I am medicated, in denial, or putting up a front. All I have to say is that God has prepared me physically and mentally for this crisis. Of course, I am heartbroken. I lost my husband and the father of our three children. I just choose not to grieve the traditional way. I wore white to his funeral and hot pink shoes to his memorial, and I kept a closed casket to remember him alive and happy. I grieve, but I do it in a way that inspires me to be a better person, a better mother, and better friend in honor of my husband. John-Marlon fought his illness with the strength of a warrior; even as he battled cancer, having fun was still on the agenda.

I am about to grieve now as I miss him dearly, and my grieving tonight means listening to "Gone, Gone, Gone." You should listen to it, too. I love this song. I need Phillip Phillips to sing this to me!

5.14.13

When John-Marlon's traditional "medical" doctor told him that he would be hospitalized for days due to his 104-degree fever, his holistic doctor adjusted him—and his fever was gone in thirty minutes. John-Marlon had so much renewed strength that he even cleaned our roof gutters the day after being bed-ridden. When the medical docs told me that John-Marlon had two weeks to live, I kept this heavy news to myself and had him see his holistic chiropractor almost every day thereafter. John-Marlon lived another five months.

Today, my five-year-old hurt her back and was in tremendous pain. Guess where we ended up? We paid a visit to our holistic chiropractor, and she is now just fine. I choose to believe that my husband sent me a message today via my daughter that I must not forget the holistic lifestyle I had adapted before his passing. I have great respect for medical doctors, but I have greater respect for the miracle workers that heal via the body's innate abilities, which are God-given.

5.14.13

I began doing the Insanity workout in March 2012. I started working out because I was in such a dark place. Due to my husband's recent diagnosis, I wanted to challenge myself mentally so I could overcome my depression. Insanity not only helped kick my depression to the curb, but I managed to lose fifty pounds and became able to deal with stress so much better.

At my husband's memorial, I had an aha moment when one of my teammates reminded me that Insanity not only prepared me mentally but it prepared me physically for the final weeks of my husband's life. Toward the end of my John-Marlon's life, he struggled physically—just as the Phillip Phillips's song says, "You're my crutch when my legs stop moving."

When John-Marlon's legs could barely move on their own, I became his crutch. I lifted him, supported him, physically moved his legs, and maneuvered his body ever so carefully. Even in the presence of other men, he refused anyone else's offer to lift him; he entrusted only me with his delicate condition.

I am just 120 pounds, but he knew I was physically strong enough to lift his heavy frame and hold him up as long as it took for him to gain his balance. Insanity not only made me one tough cookie mentally but it prepared my body like a well-oiled machine ready for battle. In the end, I lost my husband, but I gained a tremendous respect for who I am and what I am capable of. He would be proud.

5.15.13

Good morning! Before John-Marlon passed away, I was blessed enough to have a conversation with him about whether he wanted to be buried or cremated. As a couple with small children, we reasoned that we did not want them to grieve his passing standing over a tombstone for the rest of their lives, and we decided on cremation.

When I asked him what I should do with his ashes, he choked up and couldn't quite get the words out. I knew what he was going to say. He looked at me with tears running down his face and said, "Put me in the ocean."

I, of course, was an emotional mess. I asked, "Which ocean?"

He whispered, "Key West."

I responded in a joking way. "Are you serious? Not only do you want me to fly to Florida but you want me to drive five hours to Key West? Oh, you are so complicated!"

He, of course, laughed. "Wherever you want, then." He chuckled through his tears.

We eventually agreed that I would travel to Key West, and we would spread his ashes wherever there was a body of water to remember his life and his spirit.

As I told our kids, we will forever be a family of five, and Daddy will be with us wherever we go. I meant that literally. Now, instead of my kids crying over a tombstone, we will be traveling, remembering, and celebrating their dad's life in a unique and joyous way. Yesterday marked one week since I lost him. Time stands still for no one. Enjoy your life to the fullest! I, too, will try my best to do so.

5.16.13

Happy Thursday, everyone. I told my John-Marlon before he passed that I will live with purpose, and I can't think of a better way to honor his memory than to continue to share fearlessly. For a very long time, I have been praised for being a supermom, but I was secretly running on empty. I began to feel like a fraud. Autism and then cancer began to consume my world, and I needed inner healing fast. When I began to realize that the balance I was yearning for consisted of mind, body, and soul, the kinks began to work themselves out, and I soon discovered my inner sexy fabulous peace in the chaos of it all.

I consider myself a simpleton who wears my hair in a bun 99 percent of the time, bites my fingernails, and uses little makeup. Maybe I actually use four pieces of makeup. However, within that simplicity, there are many complex layers full of depth and knowledge that have helped me get through some really rough patches.

Through the grace of God, I have been able to turn those hardships into positive forces in my life. Here is a quick recap of my life in the last year. While I helped John-Marlon fight cancer, I simultaneously fought a school district for the educational needs of my son. I eventually won my case after many, many ugly and painful meetings. The fight was well worth it since the district agreed on my school of choice for the next six years of my son's school career.

After nine months of chemo (January–September) John-Marlon's health began to decline. He went from Stage 2 to Stage 4 with treatment. When I realized that chemo would eventually kill him, I began to do my own research. I spent my days working an eleven-hour shift and my nights in search for a cure.

In October, I had gathered enough research to feel confident that we needed to try a holistic approach to John-Marlon's disease. In September 2011, he was showing signs of his life coming to an end, but by October, he was playing basketball and living at 80 percent of his former self. The holistic lifestyle was indeed agreeing with him.

As I helped John-Marlon transform his life, my own transformation was taking place. I lost fifty pounds, adopted a new diet, and gained tremendous physical and mental strength.

As I have traveled a tricky road, especially in the last year, many have asked how I found my strength. There is no question that God played the starring role, but through many different mediums, he taught me how to heal. My hope is that anyone who is going through his or her own darkness can find some light in me sharing our story. I hope you join me on my future journeys, as I cannot travel this road alone. God bless you.

5.17.13

Happy Friday, my friends. I had so many thoughts brewing about what I wanted to share today with regard to what has helped my soul. I eventually made the decision, and I was ready to deliver my message—and then life happened.

In the darkness of my room, with my laptop emitting the only source of light, I heard cries. The cries carried tremendous pain, sorrow, sadness, and confusion. The cries were coming from my five-year-old daughter. She repeatedly yelled, "I want to be a baby. I want to be a baby. I want to be a baby."

By the time I ran to her room, I thought her nightmare was over, but it was no nightmare. She was alert, sitting on her bed, repeating the phrase uncontrollably for at least fifteen minutes. The more I hugged her, the more she screamed the same request. When I finally calmed her down, she whispered, "I want to be a baby so my daddy can hold me again."

My heart broke, and I found myself consoling her. I yearned for one last hug and one last smile too. For the past ten days, I have celebrated my husband's life because I understand that he is with Jesus; nevertheless, when I saw the world through the innocent eyes of my daughter, I felt my heart grow so extremely heavy. All I could do was hug her as we rocked back and forth, both yearning for what we could not have.

I so desperately wanted to tell her that the pain will lessen, but I knew that the right next step did not require words. In the days before John-Marlon passed, he was selfless enough to tell me that I too would need to move on with my life one day.

In time, I may be able to love again. In time, my little Ava may not be in such pain, but right now, neither of us is ready for those words of encouragement. I have a husband in heaven, I can't really even say the *widow* word, and my daughter misses her daddy. Sometimes our healing comes in the form of hugs, and no words need to be spoken.

Daddies and Mommies, but especially Daddies: Hug your children tighter today and every day. They will remember … and they may even remember this very moment twenty years from now.

5.18.13

I have always craved inner healing, but I never knew how to obtain it—it always seemed so complex. My husband's illness has really tested my faith, and what better time to take on this challenge of surrendering? He loaned me a beautiful soul for fifteen years. And though he has taken him back, he leaves me with so much. Praise God.

5.19.13

I am overwhelmed, overjoyed, touched, and blessed to have so many messages in my inbox sharing your own personal stories. Some of you have shared your losses as well—losses to cancer, some to accidents, some to addiction, and others to infidelity. Some women remain married, but they feel abandoned. The common thread in all of our stories is that we have lost our significant others in one way or another.

If I am going to be honest about finding inner peace, I have to be completely transparent. I am leaving my comfort zone right about now. *I can't remember the first time I met John-Marlon.* Let's just say that I kind of knew him forever, but we never said more than a casual hello. The first time we actually spoke, I offered him a drink at a bar because I had always witnessed him buying drinks for everyone else. I thought he deserved someone doing the same for him. He was alarmed that I bought him a drink, but he was even more shocked to learn that I didn't drink alcohol.

Within a few weeks, we were dating. Within six months, I was showered with amazing gifts: a jet-ski, several vacations, and a car. Even my credit cards were paid off. Oh yeah, and since he had a furniture store, he delivered new mattresses to everyone in my house. I had a well-paying job and was quite independent, but any typical twenty-two-year-old would be flattered to be pampered that way.

John-Marlon's passion was not clear to me, but his passion oozed out of his pores. He loved to please people in general; everyone who knew him would be bitten by the fun bug. John-Marlon loved when others shared his zest for life, and at the beginning of our relationship, that was all good. It was not nearly as much fun after we had our firstborn. Marken had developmental delays and eventually was diagnosed with autism. After many years of intervention—and continued support—Marken has developed beautifully. Today he is like any typical twelve-year-old, except smarter. :)

As we had our second and third children, I became more focused on structure and finances, and John-Marlon's obsessions, interests, and toys grew bigger and bigger by the year. When things spiraled out of control, I demanded that he see a neuropsychologist because I needed my suspicions confirmed.

After six hours of being evaluated, he was diagnosed with Asperger's syndrome, just like our son. Yep, my suspicions were spot on. Once he knew he had Asperger's, our marriage began to crumble super-fast because he now felt that he had a free pass to give into his obsessions and impulses.

At that point in our marriage, I think he went to the gym six times a week, played basketball three times a week, engaged in every extreme sport imaginable, played golf, and fished. He hung out with anyone who would call him. As if friends and random people calling him to hang out were not enough entertainment, John-Marlon would later confess that on nights he didn't have plans, he would literally grab his phone and scroll down his contact list. He would text and call people until someone was willing to join him on any given adventure. It makes no sense, I know, unless you understand the very complex world of living with someone with Asperger's.

These postdiagnosis years were the most awful years of our marriage. I drove him to get the diagnosis, but I did not provide him with the tools to manage, understand, and overcome it. He was devastated and lost. I was not a pillar of support after the diagnosis. I had more of an "I-told-you-so" attitude. I was mean, and my behavior was unacceptable.

After a few months of this madness, I fell into a terrible depression. I demanded a divorce. We managed not to speak for most of 2011; for three months, he completely shut down. It was as if I did not exist. My depression did not lead to lack of appetite, though; I started packing on those dreaded miserable-wife pounds.

I am a hot-blooded Latina, and when I expressed my desire for a divorce, I didn't just say it or yell it once. I was a woman scorned and enraged, and my tongue was venomous and lethal. Eventually, those luscious lips that he desired caused him to completely shut me out of his life and reject me altogether.

Somehow we managed to coparent successfully through that period. John-Marlon was an amazing father; I don't think there is one activity he did not do with his children. He was even Mr. Mom for many months when I worked a crazy shift. We were so good at pretending to be a couple that we even faked our happiness at a few events we attended.

I recall one event in particular. I was the keynote speaker at a fundraiser, that raised more than $500,000. We had to do a lot of smiling and posing that evening. We faked it until the night ended. It was clear that we had to part, but he refused to leave our family, even though I kicked him out at least a dozen times. He preferred to live as roommates than to walk away from his children.

Eventually, we experienced an intervention from God. As we slowly began to open our hearts to one another, we were struck with the biggest tragedy of our lives. Cancer made its grand entrance.

en John-Marlon was first diagnosed, there was bitterness, and confusion on his part. As for me, I was arrogant and confident that he would beat it. In my head, I assumed his inevitable wellness was a given because we were in love again! Would God take away my husband after all we had been through?

John-Marlon fought cancer for a little more than eighteen months. During this period, John-Marlon and I gave our hearts to the Lord. What the heck does that mean? I know, I know. A year ago, I would have perceived someone who said that to be a crazy Jesus-lover, full of tremendous guilt. How blind! How innocent! How sad of me! I was an empty shell living in negativity. I wanted change, but didn't know how to get out. I was trapped. My life was in such complete chaos and turmoil. I had no choice but to surrender. It was a path I saw and took and continue to walk today.

Surrendering meant putting our newfound faith first, regardless of our circumstances. The closer John-Marlon and I grew to our faith, the closer we grew to each other. In the last three months of John-Marlon's life, he emerged as my soul mate, and I was his. He told me his innermost darkest secrets; he shared the good, the bad, the ugly, and the uglier.

In one of those moments, he grabbed my hand, and with tears streaming down his face, He smiled the biggest smile—it was almost angelic—and whispered, "I forgive you." I could see in his eyes that the forgiveness was for something much deeper than just my dirty mouth.

With great concern, I asked, "For what?"

He said, "You know."

I truly did not know what he was referring to, and my heart began to sink. He had to be referring to that one night where I had blacked out. I took a deep breath and asked him to please spell out what I was being forgiven for.

He smiled and in detail explained how I betrayed our sacred home. It all started coming back to me; he actually believed everything I told him about my pretend affair. Apparently I had many—and in my very own bedroom.

Oh dear God what have I done? I don't even remember saying half the things I said I did. I felt like such an idiot—of course, he would believe me. He has Asperger's, for goodness' sake. He takes everything literally!

I looked at him, leaned over, grabbed his face, and with tears now making their way down my cheeks and onto his chest, I said, "Please believe me. I never did that." I expected a rebuttal, but I only got a bigger smile.

He said, "I believe you, but it doesn't matter. I would have forgiven you either way; forgiveness is forgiveness."

We cried and hugged. He grabbed my hand tightly and told me he had to tell me something. He not only confessed that he was the happiest man on earth knowing I had never even kissed a man outside of our marriage but he blew my mind by confessing that he had carried out his own betrayal in retaliation. He asked for forgiveness, and in the same breath, he offered any and all details of the betrayal. Although I initially felt sucker punched, I was overcome with tremendous peace just by looking into his eyes and seeing the sincerity and the pain that he carried for both of us. I told him I forgave him and the details were not important. "Forgiveness is forgiveness," I repeated as tears streamed down my face. He gently wiped them away.

After speaking for eight straight hours, we were interrupted by the alarm set for my six o'clock wake-up. He ended the conversation by sharing that he wouldn't change his journey since this journey had led him to find himself. "I love who I am, and I know who I am," he said. His lips quivered with joy, and his eyes sparkled with tears.

I knew exactly what he meant—as I too had changed—and I also loved the new and improved me. We both had peace that surpassed understanding.

In the days prior to his passing, he assured the pastor, his dear friends, and me that he was ready to be with Jesus. He smiled grandly whenever he mentioned his upcoming visit to heaven.

As I held his hand, John-Marlon took his last breath on May 7. On that day, I lost two people who were dear to me. I lost the guy who swept me off my feet with adventures, love, affection, and passion—the guy who taught me how to live in the moment and live with purpose. I also lost my soul mate, the man I fell madly in love with on a spiritual level who I had met just three months prior. He was honest, humble, emotionally connected, and present.

There were many nights in those final months that we cried together, when we both hoped for more time and prayed for God to provide us with his cure and healing, but we were at peace with God's decision. We knew that the love and the miracle we shared could not be obtained by even the happiest couples. John-Marlon took many moments to apologize for not being the husband I deserved for many years of our marriage. He was enlightened enough to understand that his limitations prohibited him from communicating effectively in our marriage, and he saw clearly that his obsessions and impulsive tendencies were extreme. Asperger's definitely played the starring role in our marriage during the rocky years.

I, too, could have been a better wife for many of those years, but nevertheless, there are no regrets. I am the woman I am today because of my experiences. I am honored and blessed that God chose me to travel this road with him. God placed us together so that we could live our most fulfilled life through lessons that will transcend far beyond the two of us—and be shared, just as I am doing now.

John-Marlon was so selfless and beautiful. He reminded me that I must move on and continue my life. He said he wanted me to remarry and be treated in the most exceptional way. Tears streamed down his face when he shared how he expected a man to treat our children in the future. He cried and smiled when he thought of all the time we lost, as we allowed the chaos and noise of the world around us to interrupt the bonding that could have been. We had fun and were madly in love with each other for fifteen years, but pride, the art of surrendering, and the absence of faith, spirituality, and God in our hearts made many of those years unnecessarily painful.

In the end, John-Marlon and I agreed that this is the way our story was meant to end. We had a fairytale ending as far as I'm concerned. I fell in love twice with the man I married. I have no doubt we shall meet again and continue right where we left off.

I wouldn't change my journey for the world. I am who I am because of it—every single bit of it!

5.20.13

I miss watching *Duck Dynasty, Deadliest Catch,* and *Pawn Stars* with John-Marlon. Hug your loved ones tonight—tomorrow is not promised. I can now say I speak from experience. Night, night.

5.21.13

Oh boy. Feeling the heaviness in my heart. Tomorrow, I will be closing the business my husband ran for twenty years. This furniture store was his baby. It meant so much that he didn't give me the green light to shut it down until two days before he passed away. Although I would make one darn cute salesperson, I must focus on what I do best so I can provide for my children. I never thought this would break my heart to do. I am taking a deep breath, knowing Steinway Street will never be the same.

Going to sleep at three o'clock in the morning for the last couple of nights is definitely not in line with how I would tell others to live their lives, but as of tonight, that changes. My days are busy with unraveling legal issues. Death can be like a divorce: pretty messy and not what I would call fun. Argh.

5.23.13

Before John-Marlon passed away, I told anyone who would listen that I would *never* marry or be in a serious relationship. I was done with relationships. I just wanted to enjoy life and my children.

As many of you know, John-Marlon encouraged me to keep an open heart and fall in love again, and he shared how he wanted my future partner to treat our children and me. I thought he was off his rocker, but he was in fact a man ahead of his time.

I had a breakthrough at midnight last night; I do deserve another shot at love. I can begin to accept that I do have permission to move on with my life one day. I am by no means ready (no applications please), but my husband is giving me so much comfort that I feel his presence at this very moment. I am never alone.

5.23.13

I know I promised to be in bed early these days, but I just had tea with a dear friend who also attends my church. I feel so renewed—so healed—after our affirming conversation. There was heaviness in my heart that I could not let go that secretly surfaced two days ago. I was being haunted by the thought of his betrayal, and I wanted him to come out at night and haunt me so that I could curse him out one last time. *How could he? Maybe I do want details.*

After my three-hour conversation with my friend, I have never felt so clear about my present relationship with my husband. My journey is meant to show healing and inner peace here on earth to others, and John-Marlon is my protector who will guide me to fulfill my purpose in life. I probably sound like I have lost my mind, but I have never been so sure of anything. I received way too many signs today that he is lighting the pathway of my life, and looking back is not part of this most glorious plan.

5.24.13

My apologies if you have sent me a message and I have not gotten back to you. I have indeed read all of your messages and took a few hours last week to respond to most of you. I will do the same in the next couple of days. I am humbled, honored, and blessed to have so many listening to my cries, celebrating my glory, and rooting for me.

To everyone who donated to my children's college fund in lieu of flowers, you rock! The flowers that were graciously bought by my cousin for the casket were thrown out the moment we left the funeral home. She refused to let me pay. If ever you are going to send flowers to a funeral, check first if the deceased's children can benefit from a donation. Flowers die. Education is for a lifetime.

5.25.13

Happy Friday. Today I rushed my kids all morning because we were up late due to recital practice. I noticed that my rushing changed my girls' moods significantly. Our energy affects those around us, including children, whether we realize it or not. I don't like it when someone throws his or her heavy energy my way. I am an expert at *boomeranging* someone's bad energy back to that person and avoiding it altogether; however, children do not have a choice when they are on the receiving end. I will do better in this area. We're still getting into the rhythm of our new lives.

5.25.13

There was much chaos and too many interruptions for most of our relationship, but in the end, we were just as we were meant to be—just the two of us as I watched his chest rise and fall when he took his last breath. I get chills thinking of him calling my name the entire night before he passed. I finally accept that I was his everything, and just in case he doesn't know it, he is mine.

5.25.13

As it rains in New York City, I am thinking of my rain angel and our wedding day. The crowd gathered around us with their hands clasped, waiting for our first dance as a couple. And then to their surprise, we danced a *perico ripiao*. For those of you that don't know what it that is, it's a fast-spinning, crazy-turning, hip-shaking art form of a dance when you are in perfect sync with your partner—and that we were! It was one heck of an awesome intro to our lives together as husband and wife. We ultimately did dance a slow song, "Lady in Red," which John-Marlon chose.

5.26.13

Thanks to my sis, I motivated myself to clean out the garage. John-Marlon couldn't stand when I used the garage as a dumping ground. Now, I can see why. He would be so proud of me. I donated eight bags of clothes, and per his instructions, I gave his snow blower, power washer, and smoker grill to our neighbor and his family who watch over me and our children like personal bodyguards. They know my every move, and I am so grateful. John-Marlon left me in peace, knowing I would be protected in many ways. More than anything, he is my virtual protector. God is good!

5.27.13

If you feel the urge to tell someone that it's okay to grieve, trust me that she's already gotten the memo. Please remind that person not to lose hope and to take one day at a time. That is much more helpful than most standard, inane comments.

My journey has taught me that sometimes words are not necessary if you don't know what to say. It's hard to empathize with someone unless you have experienced a similar loss. I am guilty of vomiting— oops, I meant saying—the wrong words to someone, but I am more mindful these days. I grieve as I stop to smell the roses, look at the blue sky, admire the rain, appreciate my children's laughter, and listen to love songs. I grieve every second of the day, but the joy in my heart manages to surpass the pain. I have peace beyond understanding.

5.28.13

Going through John-Marlon's text messages is like reading the thoughts from my secret crush. He was the guy who, throughout our relationship, enjoyed watching me sleep—because he thought I was beautiful. He always craved my attention, and he always wanted me by his side.

There are not many text messages prior to his last two months because we were glued to each other's hips. I'm smiling because he has amazing things in store for me. I know it. Lying in bed alone is not depressing; it's actually comforting. He hasn't left my side and never will.

5.30.13

I visited a high school friend who is battling cancer in the hospital. Another friend babysat my kids at the last minute, and what a day they had. While I was stuck in traffic for almost four hours round-trip, it didn't bother me one bit because I was just grateful to be alive. I lost my husband, but I'm still breathing—and I am here. Today was yet another reminder that our days are numbered. Life is beautiful. Open your eyes—even if through the tears. Be grateful, and be humbled by the miracle of you.

6.1.13

Today someone pissed me off, ugh, and I was not very Christlike. In the future, I will sleep and pray on something that bothers me before letting my emotions take charge. People who let other people's actions affect their emotions most definitely live toxic lives. I chose a year ago not to be one of those people, and shame on me for my slipup.

Wherever you go, there you are. It's best to be at peace with your actions and most importantly your reactions! I forget I'm human! Argh!

6.2.13

John-Marlon's store is officially closed. Great memories in Astoria! Sometimes, you have to let go and hold on to memories. At eighteen years of age, he opened his first business, and for the next twenty years, he would continue in the same line of business. He went from one-thousand-square-foot store in Astoria, Queens, which he stocked with a sea of mattresses, to ten thousand square feet of really cool modern furniture in the Bronx.

6.3.13

Tears stream down my face as I take my first look at his closet. Basketball jerseys, fins … and this is not even his activity closet! I wish I would have been more into fitness so that we could have had this as a common ground during our rough patch. When he could no longer work out, he motivated me to keep pushing my body. I won't lose sight of that now that he is gone. I guess the walk-in closet with the window is now mine, but it's not the way I wanted to have it.

6.4.13

The night John-Marlon passed away, I went shopping at eight o'clock for my white suit and white dress for his funeral and celebration. I have no idea how someone like me, who hates shopping, found the strength to shop the very day he died. The following day, on May 8, I went shopping for him. I could not fathom putting a suit on my husband since he was such a sports fanatic. Instead, I decided to buy him a Giants jersey.

I chose not to use one of his own because I want to save those for our son. I went to Modell's, but I couldn't figure out which Giants player was the most popular. I decided to ask one of the workers. I went up to the gentlemen and asked for help. He looked at me, quite annoyed, and I could feel his negative energy suffocating me.

When I asked him to help me pick out a popular jersey, he said, "Why don't you ask the person you're buying it for?"

I looked at him with compassion and said, "You know, I wish I could, but it's for my husband. This is what he is wearing to his funeral."

It turned out the gentleman who was helping me was the store manager. As his eyes welled up with sadness, he apologized and said, "I thought today was the saddest day of my life until you shared that." He said he had to let go of an employee who was like his daughter on that very day. He also apologized for being rude.

I said, "She will be okay if I can survive my husband's death. And you will be okay. Surrender your worries to God, and he will take care of it."

As I checked out, he gave me his manager's discount. Today, I went back to the sporting goods store to buy my gear for the Spartan race. As I walked in, the manager ran up to me and greeted me with a warm smile. He not only remembered who I was, but he informed me that the employee he had let go had visited the store for the first time that day. He pointed to her right behind me. She was high-fiving the other employees and telling them how happy she was to be unemployed since her unemployment check was more than she was making at the store.

"I thank you for affecting my life in such a positive way," he said. "I will never forget you." And with that, he walked me up to the cashier and gave me his manager's discount—again.

6.6.13

I am surprising Ava at school today! Here is another eerie magical moment we are experiencing after John-Marlon's passing. He told me he wanted to buy Ava a motor car.

Ava told me two days ago that her dad wanted her to "have" a car. I assumed they spoke about this. Later that day, Ava said, "Mom, please don't get mad. I lied. Dad never said he would buy me a car, but I know he would want me to have one." It was just magical! He is with us. No question. No doubt! She ended up getting the pink Cadillac. Daddy must have told her to pick out the most expensive one.

6.7.13

Today marks one month since my soul mate passed away. Do I ever have to pinch myself to make sure that he is gone? No. I accept his passing. Our story was written way before we ever met. As his friend Brian said at his memorial celebration, "John-Marlon would have gotten cancer with or without you in his life—thank God it was with you."

I feel so blessed that God chose me to be John-Marlon's wife. I would not be the woman I am today if it weren't for the lessons John-Marlon taught me through his life, by his death, and beyond.

On Tuesday, April 30, I had to do one of the hardest things I have ever done. I had to tell my husband he was dying. I had been told since January that he had two weeks to live, but I kept this heavy news to myself because I did not have the heart to put this weight on his shoulders. John-Marlon ended up living another five months, and in those months, we took the kids sledding in the Poconos with friends. He also took a relaxing trip to Florida to spend time with his childhood friends, Brian and Hyung. Most importantly, we emerged as soul mates.

What I am about to share may seem kind of amusing—so don't feel badly if you chuckle. I still laugh when I think about it. The reason I had to tell him that he had two weeks to live was because he was a phone call away from having a mega-pool installed in our backyard. He was disturbed that I kept delaying the project, begging me to budge because he was becoming desperate to take a swim. Can you imagine? A dying man—thinking about swimming and enjoying life!

Once the words escaped my lips, I saw the devastation on his face immediately. We cried together for a very long time. We hugged gently since he was so fragile—and I did not want to hurt him. After I shared this news, I had to follow with even more heartbreaking news. I told him that I wanted to put him in the hospice program at Calvary Hospital. I explained that I wanted to be his wife and not his caregiver. I no longer wanted to run up and down the stairs frantically. I wanted to be by his side and bond with him since we both had to come to terms that the end was near.

Seconds after I said this, his face transformed. The only way to describe it was angelic. "I'm ready to go," he said.

For the first time, I experienced inner peace; when he responded, I knew that he was ready to go to Calvary—and he was surrendering to God's will. We locked eyes and knew we would both be okay. I asked for permission to take a picture; we both gave big cheesy smiles and kissed.

Here is a timeline of his days in hospice:

4.30.13 (Tuesday)

John-Marlon was admitted as a patient. Once he arrived and got settled, he smiled. "Why didn't you put me here sooner?" The nurses broke out in laughter, and so did I.

5.1.13 (Wednesday)

Our children visited and cried terribly when they saw their father in a hospital bed. I figured this was the last time they would ever see him. I took lots of pictures and recorded John-Marlon's final messages that we will cherish forever. John-Marlon was in great spirits that day, and eventually so were the kids. My five-year-old called Calvary the "Fun Hospital."

5.2.13 (Thursday)

John-Marlon still looked good and strong. I went home and spent time with the kids, but when I returned in the evening, he said, "If you keep leaving, you're going to miss my last breath." I decided I needed to stay put.

5.3.13 (Friday)

John's health began to decline, and Pastor Dan came by to see his friend. He blessed him and anointed him with oil, and we prayed over him. We prayed for healing, but John-Marlon responded, "I'm ready to go." He was smiling.

That night, John-Marlon got a burst of energy, and we ended up watching the Knicks game together. I recorded him yelling, "Take him out" and "Kill the clock" at the TV. I had to chuckle that this guy had days to live and was still pissed off at the Knicks! I was so thankful that he was 100 percent present in his final days.

5.4.13 (Saturday)

His childhood friends visited after midnight due to a late flight. Although I insisted they not come, I was so happy that they did.

As they walked in, they were alarmed to see his state of health. Both of his friends broke down in inconsolable crying.

"I can't stand it when people are like boo-hoo-hoo. Do me a favor: Don't cry when you come see me," John-Marlon said.

Despite the seriousness of the moment, we all broke out in laughter because he meant every word of it. He did not want anyone feeling sorry for him. As the boys reminisced for the next couple of hours, we ended up laughing so hard that I thought we were going to get kicked out of his room. Instead, a nurse walked in and joined the party. It was now almost two o'clock. Later that day, John-Marlon and I had some private time and said cheers to life as we sipped white zinfandel.

5.5.13 (Sunday)

John-Marlon's renewed energy and vitality gave me "permission" to run home to get the kids to see their dad for the final time. They were so happy to see him, and I made a conscious decision to take more pictures to remind them in years to come that in their dad's final days, he was happy, present, at peace. We even posed for a silly picture. I am very happy we captured that moment because it's a reminder that he was in great spirits till the very end.

It was hard to send the kids home because I knew they would never see him again. On that night, he began to reach upward. He was semiconscious. He could barely move his body, but his intention was so purposeful that he used every ounce of his strength to reach for whatever he saw that I didn't. I knew whatever he saw was divine.

5.6.13 (Monday)

John-Marlon's health began to decline; he became restless and seemed to want only me in his presence. I told him that the following afternoon, I would need to leave him at around two o'clock to be present for our girls' recital pictures.

He looked at me and responded, "Okay, we'll see."

It was as if he knew something I didn't. For most of the rest of that day, he slept. That night, I slept next to him as I always did. I had my body on the cot and rested my head next to his on the bed since he wanted to feel my touch. Before I completely passed out, I noticed that he once again reached for something that was above him, and now he was desperate to get a hold of it.

Something happened to me that night that I still cannot explain. I felt in my heart that it was his final night, but something restrained my body from being able to get up and watch over him.

He called my name for what seemed like hours, but for every time he called my name, I could only slightly raise my head toward him and mumble, "I'm here."

He would pat my head every time I responded to his call. I tried my best to stay up and watch him, but my body was no longer being controlled by me—something had taken over. Yes, I was tired, but this had nothing to do with my inability to stay up. Every time I tried to raise my body or my head, a force pushed me back down on his bed. I still cannot explain that force. The only thing I could think of is that I was not meant to witness his final conscious moments.

5.7.13 (8:00 a.m.)

When I woke up, I was completely saddened to see he was unresponsive. I gave him a gentle kiss and called for the nurse. When the nurse came in, I said, "He will pass this morning."

She said, "He could stay like this for days."

I looked at her and said, "Call the doctor to tell him he is going this morning."

9:00 a.m.

I texted family and friends to inform them that John-Marlon would will be leaving us this morning.

11:02 a.m.

I pulled out my phone and recorded us touching hands as beautiful healing music played in the background. I put my hand on a cross in the room, placed it on him, and gave him permission to leave me. I counted six seconds in between his very heavy, labored breaths. Then there was a seven-second pause between each breath. I waited for eight seconds, but he was constant at seven seconds.

11:21 a.m.

I turned around to repeat a song on the CD player. I had my back turned for a few seconds only. Before I turned back around, I could hear that he had stopped breathing. I swiftly turned around, and with confidence and faith, I tapped his hand. I whispered, "Hey, that's not fair. I turned around for a few seconds; you can't do that. You have to give me one more breath ... one more."

I waited with faith, and it happened—with the softest blow, as if he was puckering for a kiss, he exhaled the longest sweetest breath. I swear I even heard it. It was a miracle. I smiled because he had given me one of the greatest gifts I could ever receive in this lifetime; he let me hold his hand as he took his final breath.

Before I called for the nurse, I took a moment to appreciate my life with this beautiful man and smiled. Thank you, God.

6.8.13

Wow! I did my best ... four obstacles out of twenty-five destroyed me, but P90X will fix that for next race. I only decided to enter this race after John-Marlon passed so my training was definitely not enough, but I gave it my all! Thank you for rooting for me. Everyone should experience a good old butt-whippin' Spartan race at some point.

6.9.13

After my daughter's final soccer game of the season, the most beautiful butterfly fluttered around Natalia's hair. It didn't want to leave her side until she waved it away. As the butterfly flew away from Natalia, he made a purposeful beeline to my younger daughter and ended up landing on her. There were at least a dozen people gathered in a circle, but the butterfly only touched Natalia and Ava. It was pretty awesome, and not until another mom pointed it out, did I realize how special that moment was.

As we walked into the ice cream parlor to celebrate the final game of the season, my son walked in ahead of the group. He quickly returned to announce that "Gone, Gone, Gone" was playing. John-Marlon has mastered his communication skills!

My kids were all touched by their dad today, and that was amazing, but I also secretly wanted to experience my own connection.

At the ice cream parlor, one of the parents mentioned that I should keep an eye out for the red cardinal.

I said, "Funny you say that because my two cousins mentioned this morning that a red cardinal kept presenting itself days after John-Marlon's passing. I, in turn, told them that I never notice such things, but I, too, have seen the cardinal visit and frequently just sit on my deck."

Today, since my kids had a direct connection to their dad, I decided I wanted one too. As soon as I got home, I ran out of my car, opened my backyard door, and whistled. I knew in my heart that I would see what I was looking for.

In less than a minute, I could hear its beautiful whistle. I did not have the chance to zoom in when I captured the moment with my phone camera, but I could make out the red in the middle of all the green. Some say that the cardinal is symbolic of peace after death, and others believe it is a loved one visiting you. I don't like to think of my husband as a bird, so I will go with the first door and say it symbolizes peace after death. Either way, I do love seeing the mysterious ways that cardinals continue to show up in our lives. I firmly believe it is communication from beyond.

6.10.13

Don't let your pride get in the way of your friendship or love. The Bible says, "He that humbles himself will be exalted." Humble yourself, and make peace with someone today.

John-Marlon had many acquaintances, but very few true friends. One of his profound friendships was with someone who was also one of my very good friends. Back in 1996, I had a friend by the name of Angel, and coincidentally, he was John-Marlon's good friend too. Although I had known John-Marlon for years, we had never spoken. John-Marlon was actually friends with my ex-boyfriend. I know this sounds scandalous, but before your imagination runs wild, I was single for two years before we became a couple.

Angel used to have terrific house parties every other weekend. At those parties, I used to show up with my still-best-friend Carol, and John-Marlon always seemed to have a different girl on his arm. The girls always looked the same: beautiful, tiny waists, and worthy of being put in a storefront window as a mannequin. We never, ever spoke during Angel's parties. We were so different. I was hip-hop, and he was cumbia!

At John-Marlon's memorial celebration, Angel spoke of the memories of his dear friend. Although it was in Spanish, he had the entire room cracking up. His story was so heartfelt and ridiculously funny that the laughter was contagious.

Due to John-Marlon's Asperger's, he was very black and white. There was absolutely no gray with him. It was hard for him to connect with people unless it was in a sports or social environment that did not require a lot of talking. So many people had the wrong perception of John-Marlon, just as I did when I would see him at Angel's parties. John-Marlon wore his heart on his sleeve; it was his way or no way. He had absolutely no filter, was obsessive about his passions, and sometimes his honesty was too much for most to handle.

Many questioned why Angel would put up with John-Marlon's difficult personality. Angel would always come to his defense and brush off people by saying, "You just don't understand him."

When John-Marlon was diagnosed with Asperger's in 2010, the first call he made after we left the clinic was to Angel. He was very emotional and could not believe that he was on the autism spectrum just like our son. He shared with Angel that although he was shocked to receive such a diagnosis, he was happy that he finally had a name for his "way of being." He reflected on his childhood as he spoke to his friend, and his eyes welled with tears, knowing it now all made sense. I watched from the passenger seat, wondering if I had made a mistake by pushing him to get a diagnosis.

Angel and John-Marlon were friends for almost twenty years, but they were more like brothers. As we blossomed into adulthood, we went on vacations together and spent holidays as a family. Angel's wife, Kathy, said, "We are a couple of four, not two." We were inseparable.

The moment the clock struck midnight and everyone cheered for the New Year—in 2012—I ran into Angel and Kathy's bathroom. I locked myself inside and cried uncontrollably. I didn't even hug my family because I was completely broken and sad.

Once Kathy convinced me to let her in the bathroom, I yelled in tremendous pain that John-Marlon had cancer. He had not been diagnosed yet, but I knew it! We both cried and hugged each other as if he had already passed away. I knew in my heart that we had a tough fight ahead of us.

As the months passed, John-Marlon became weaker, and I became stronger. I began to work out and eat differently. I joined a fitness team and adopted a totally new lifestyle. John-Marlon cheered me every step of the way; he was so proud. He couldn't work out, but he didn't allow me into bed unless I had completed mine. He was living vicariously through me, and he was showing tremendous support for anything and everything that I wanted to do.

As I was posting my every move on Facebook, some people did not quite understand my newfound passion for fitness in the midst of my husband's illness. Angel and his family became overly concerned that my lifestyle was leaving me less time for John-Marlon whose health was declining by the day. I was devastated by the number of people who were offended by me taking one hour a day to work out, and it began to take an emotional toll.

John-Marlon was livid that anyone would judge me when I was working a full-time job, fighting a school district, acting as his driver and caregiver, and parenting three kids. He insisted that I could really piss people off if I went to Vegas for a Beachbody Conference with my fitness team. I didn't want to go that far, but he insisted that if I didn't go, I was not living my life with purpose, as he wanted me to. He even helped me choose my outfits for the trip.

We were in a very fragile place, beginning to tap into our faith, and confused about who the toxic people were in our lives, and who was concerned. Because we could not clearly identify the good from the bad, we severed ties with anyone who said anything that weighed heavily on us—and that included Angel and Kathy. John-Marlon was very protective of me, and if he felt that someone hurt my feelings, he wanted nothing to do with them. Twenty years of friendship was flushed down the toilet. We tossed away that friendship from April 2012 until January 2013.

Pride on both sides prevented the relationship from mending sooner. However, when I knew that John-Marlon had limited time, I called Angel to tell him we needed to fix things as soon as possible. Kathy reminded me that we will always remain "a couple of four."

In those final months, Angel was a true angel to his friend. Angel came over and watched sports with John-Marlon, just as John-Marlon had taught him to learn to appreciate. They went to the movies and to eat together; as John-Marlon's health dramatically declined, their friendship was more rooted than ever.

In John-Marlon's final weeks, Angel would come to our house and—as if it was part of his visiting duties—he would shave him, apply lotion to his hands, and put John-Marlon's feet on his lap and massage them for what seemed like hours. There was a silent exchange of gratitude. John-Marlon would direct Angel and tell him where he enjoyed Angel's touch the most.

Angel said, "I will do whatever you want—except happy endings."

They were hilarious! I thought the massages were as intimate as two friends could get, until I witnessed one of the most beautiful bonds between friends that I had ever seen.

I was the only person allowed to help John-Marlon with a bath, but on this particular day, he looked at Angel and said, "Angel, help me take a bath." This makes me quite emotional because I know why John-Marlon did it. John-Marlon wanted Angel to be at peace with the lost time that had passed by—to know that there were no hard feelings.

Angel had never seen how fragile John-Marlon was up until this point. Only I knew what he looked like beneath his clothing. When Angel pulled off John-Marlon's shirt, I could see the look of sadness and pain on his face, even though he tried to hide it.

With the most gentle hands and care, Angel lathered his hands and washed his old friend's hair. Angel continued on to his fragile skeletal body.

John-Marlon was still wearing his underwear and warned Angel to not even think about washing his privates. We all laughed, and that broke the awkward silence. As Angel took a bucket and poured it over John-Marlon's head, you could see the joy it brought to both to experience this simple pleasure. As water trickled down John-Marlon's face, which showcased his tremendous smile and big, beautiful green eyes, he projected so much love and gratitude for the friendship that will always remain.

6.12.13

I just found a note with the word *sorry*. I can't remember why I was upset at my hubby, but when I pulled into the driveway after running errands one day, he called out my name from the upstairs window. He held a sign up in front of his face. As I walked in, I could smell the aroma of his cooking. He greeted me with the deepest, sincere kiss, pulled out my chair, and served me my favorite shrimp dish.

I miss his cooking, his smile, his eyes, his touch, and his incredible love for me. As I sat in bed just now, I began to cry, thinking of the incredible love that man had for me, but I just couldn't see it. I probably just said a sarcastic "thanks" after his incredible efforts to make me happy after this silly argument. It was hard for me to love him unconditionally, but I thank God I was able to show him during our final months together. I am so happy he saw the real me … my heart at its purest … my love with no walls.

As I sat in bed just now, Ava, our six-year-old, screamed for her dad. She must have felt my energy. Loving is easy; we just make it complicated. Seriously, people, if you're going to love, love all the way. Don't half-ass it. Forgiving and asking for forgiveness does not mean you lost the battle; it means you have won in love! It's going to be tough tonight, folks, but tomorrow will be better because John-Marlon didn't like me to cry. So: two nights in a row, he ain't gonna have that! Tomorrow will be an awesome day.

6.12.13

My baby had her moving-up ceremony today. Ava wanted to wear the same dress she wore to her preschool graduation because her daddy loved it so much. Ava was the last one presented with her certificate and got the loudest cheers. So sweet. I am so grateful for all of the support. I was too emotional to even call out her name. Marken presented Ava with flowers on behalf of Daddy.

6.13.13

Some have said my husband has possessed me because I am a different person. I sure am! We were stuck in traffic for five hours, and my sis, mom, nephew, and kids laughed all the way. No stress! "Gone, Gone, Gone" played on the radio twice, and "Mirrors" by Justin Timberlake (my other favorite song) played at least seven times. John is forever my mirror staring back at me. He keeps me line with living a life with purpose.

We have arrived at one of John-Marlon's favorite destinations to bring the kids: Great Wolf Lodge. The kids have three beds and a fireplace in their private bunk-bed, pool-view suite! Off to do what I now do best: have fun!

6.15.13

Quickie vacation over! We will be back in time for the Father's Day service at my church. I thought about keeping the kids away for Father's Day, but their dad being gone is something that will never go away. We must face this, our first Father's Day, without Daddy. If we make it this year, we will survive every year hereafter.

6.16.13

Happy Father's Day to all dads! Your role is forever marked in the hearts of your children. For the daddies who barely get a passing grade on fatherhood, it's never too late to make good. Make today the day that you see the world through the eyes of your children. For all of the men who step in as male role models when fathers are absent, God bless you. For all my single mommies out there, we got this! As I have been told, God gives his toughest battles to his strongest soldiers. We have been chosen! Have a blessed day!

Happy Father's Day in heaven, honey. Before the kids went to bed last night, we had a family talk about you. You know the details, so you can imagine how heartbreaking it was for me to watch them cry for you. I pray that you will give the kids tremendous strength to get through the day today.

As for me, when my heart aches for your love, I play the song we both silently loved and listened to during those difficult months in February and March as we commuted to the hospital—"Gone, Gone, Gone." Even months before you said goodbye, I knew this would be the song that would offer me healing. I now know all of the words and belt it out as I envision you and I singing our parts perfectly to one another—you from heaven and me on earth. I love you.

6.18.13

Many, many thanks to everyone for the sincere support and continued surprises for my children during this most difficult time. My kids came home to a card and a signed football from the New York Giants.

If you hear thunder in New York City, that is John-Marlon's insanely loud cheering. God is abundant in his grace and mercy. No one chooses when he or she will be born or when he or she will die. I lost my husband way too young, but his memory continues to live on through moments like this. He was a big-time Giants fan—so much so that I dressed him in a Giants jersey for his funeral.

Do you guys see the rain in New York City? That's my rain angel showering his blessings upon us. Be grateful even through the difficult times. God will amaze you. Take it one day at a time. That's what I do. That is all we can do.

6.19.13

After an emotional day at the pool watching my baby girl do what daddy taught her best—to be a little fish—I decided at the last minute to get my laugh on at Stand Up NY. Absolutely no traffic. I am here with my BFF who is so happy I took some mommy time. Nice to have comedians as friends who make you laugh.

6.20.13

John-Marlon is touching people even through his passing. I have chills, and it's so eerie. I had three people tell me they have seen John-Marlon's name come across their desks for one reason or another. He's making his rounds! I wonder what message he is trying to convey to the recipient.

On another note, I am totally not watching the basketball game. I get too emotional watching one of John-Marlon's biggest passions, especially by myself. His many trophies in the basement bring me back to the day in October 2011 when he came home from playing and said he was having trouble breathing. From that day forward, our lives changed forever.

6.20.13

Since Father's Day, I have been extremely emotional during the day, but my evenings are still full of tremendous peace and comfort. The skylight in my bedroom (that I never quite appreciated before) affords me a perfect view of stars, the moon, and the sky. I relax and sometimes imagine John-Marlon looking back at me.

Since I have had time to reflect, I have come to the understanding that there is no way around it—marriage is work. It's alarming that we work on every other aspect of our lives, but many times, we neglect the one aspect, the one relationship, that many times defines us and/or breaks us to the core.

Every marriage deserves a fighting chance, but even for those marriages that are beyond repair, no one should part without dignity. Separation and divorce can feel like a death, and regardless of the cause of our empty hearts, our lives continue—and they will once again be whole.

Consider it a new opportunity to be able to live your best life! I am so grateful that even through the gray pockets of our thirteen-year marriage, we were able to experience a most amazing life together with our three beautiful children. John-Marlon packed a lifetime of memories into the very short time we knew him. As much as I valued my life with the family that once was, I wholeheartedly believe that new and precious memories will emerge.

6.21.13

I had my trip booked for Vegas this week to attend a conference with my Beachbody family, and then John-Marlon passed away. I began to have second thoughts about whether I should leave my children so soon after his death. I literally began to pray and asked for a sign from God or John-Marlon about whether I should attend.

In that very sitting, I opened my laptop and began to respond to e-mails from friends offering me condolences. As I went through my inbox, I came across an e-mail from a Stage IV cancer survivor, Kris Carr, who I had been following for a year:

> Join me for a writers' workshop in New York City on how to write your own story! One person in this workshop will have their book published and potentially even be a *NY Times* bestseller!

There was my sign! The workshop I will be attending tomorrow with four prestigious authors is happening the very weekend I should have been in Vegas. So for all of you who have encouraged me to consider writing a book, I am listening! I pray that the work I submit in January will be the chosen one for publication. Vegas will have to wait until next year because God and John-Marlon had different plans for me this weekend.

I know my obsession with Phillip Phillips is a little much, but John-Marlon is reassuring me that he is thinking of us. We are eating right now, and the song comes on. We get in the car, and there is the song. I get an e-mail confirming my meet-and-greet with Phillip Phillips, and as I am reading the e-mail, the song comes on. Yes, I am meeting Phillip Phillips! Details are forthcoming. Dreams come true. God is good.

6.22.13

Day one of my workshop was *awesometacious*. I know … I went to a writers' workshop, and now I'm using a word that does not exist. I met some terrific people. If I am going to brand myself, I need to market *me*. I just bought my new domain name: Kenianunez. com (glad it was available).

I am tickled, but I realize I need some serious structure in my life to make this dream come to life. I am a single mommy, and although I should really keep a nine-to-five job, my heart tells me I have a different calling. My mind, body, and soul are officially under construction! Let's do this! And I do mean let *us*! I can't do it alone. I need you. I hope you're having a *fantabulous* day!

Loving this moment! Kris Carr has been living with Stage IV cancer for ten years. Her journey inspired John-Marlon in so many ways once he was diagnosed. It was an honor to meet her today, and we even shared a few tears. Today is the beginning of building something—I'm not sure what exactly—but I know God has greatness in store. I am overwhelmed with joy and excitement at what is yet to come.

6.23.13

A neighbor innocently asked, "How's John?" The gaping hole in my heart was exposed today. Ouch—those two words really hurt.

6.23.13

I sneaked out of my writers' workshop because I needed one more picture with Kris. So many people have helped transform my life. Kris Carr is most definitely one of them. I predict a lunch with Kris next year over green juice and salad! I'm putting it out there, God and John-Marlon. No pressure.

Today's workshop was not about becoming an exceptional writer; it was about God's divine plan for each of us. We all have a story to tell, and no one can tell that story in a unique voice except the storyteller. If our stories change one life, that is all that matters. We all have goals, but a practical game plan without spirituality will eventually lead straight into a brick wall.

When practical action meets God's energy, an explosion of greatness occurs. I don't need to have a background in writing; there are editors for all that jazz. I am a storyteller. I have clarity. Thank you, God.

6.25.13

I'm smiling because I finally took a day for myself. Teeth cleaned: check. Physical and OB/GYN: check. In perfect health. Thank you, God.

I'm not trying to give you TMI, but I haven't checked myself in two years because I was so worried about John-Marlon's health. Cancer and other chronic illnesses do not creep up overnight. Check yourself. John-Marlon got alopecia twice—years before he was diagnosed with cancer—but instead of us doing something about his level of stress (which caused alopecia), it was more important to make sure his beautiful thick hair grew back to what it was, which it did. While he exhibited perfect health on paper, we ignored many warning signs along the way.

Moral of the story: Get your medical checkups, but also take preventative measures! Changing your lifestyle with exercise and proper nutrition is preventative medicine, and it's much cheaper than the hundreds of thousands of dollars it costs to fight the worst monster of all: cancer.

6.27.13

The obstacles that exist in our lives, the chains that hold us back from living our most fulfilled lives, are not due to bad luck—they are manifested by the very person who is reading this. You! The energy that breathes life into our souls is either having an attitude of gratitude or living life with regret and bitterness. The choice is truly yours.

I am a widow left with three small children. I have every excuse in the book to feel sorry for myself, to have anger, to have questions, and to have regrets, but I choose not to live in that space. I am grateful for John-Marlon's life, but I can also accept that his purpose was fulfilled in God's eyes in his short thirty-nine years. In his death, I have learned to love myself to the fullest. I have learned to live life with purpose, to be fearless on a case-by-case basis, and to be fierce. I even know how to be a better wife! I like to think he occupies space in my soul; actually, I know he does. He should seriously consider paying me some virtual rent! For real!

In the months prior to his passing, three completely different and unaffiliated doctors confirmed that he would die from drowning. The retention of fluid in his feet was rapidly rising to his legs, and making its way to his lungs. John-Marlon did not drown; he went in his sleep peacefully with no pain, and he gave me his last breath upon my request. I asked, and I received.

Asking without faith is like receiving without giving. God is in full control. We all know that, but we tend to forget. We tend to be control freaks, and then we question why things never or always happen to us, depending on the circumstance. God's delay does not mean a denial. Be patient, but be purposeful. Don't stand on the sidelines of life waiting for it to get better. Go ahead and give yourself permission to live with purpose. Get out of your own way.

No matter what you are encountering this very second in your life—may it be as simple as wanting to lose weight or as complex as illness—just stop. Stop and have an attitude of gratitude even if for just one minute today. Raise your head to the heavens and thank God for this very moment, for the life that he breathes into you. Surrender.

6.28.13

I have recently started flexing my faith muscle and trusting that minimiracles will happen as long as I am open to receiving them.

Last Friday was a confirmation. I had put it out into the universe that one of my biggest desires was to meet Phillip Phillips to share how "Gone, Gone, Gone" has been a healing force for my family. I had no idea how I would meet a rock star, but my faith told me I didn't have to know. I just had to ask and be open to receiving.

We hear it from the most amazing spiritual leaders and teachers that a vision board will allow us to see our dreams manifest. I can tell you that it's true! I didn't have a physical vision board, but my vision board was a virtual one in my head. I envisioned our meeting, and I even rehearsed what I would say to him.

Keeping focused on making this dream happen really kept me in a good place because I had something to look forward to. How could I mourn when I knew that God was going to line up the stars for me to meet a man who has been an inspiration of hope? I had no doubt because I had faith. In less than a month, I got the notice that my kids and I would be meeting with Phillips on *The Today Show*.

It was a most magical experience to watch him perform, but meeting him and having one-to-one time—even if just for a few minutes—was a dream come true. Everything I had rehearsed that I wanted to say completely escaped me, and I have no clue what crazy things came out of my mouth. I wasn't a groupie; I was just overwhelmed with complete and utter joy. I will cherish this experience for the rest of my life.

At this juncture, my children have incredible peace in their hearts. They are spiritually connected and know that their father has never left their sides, and now they also know that dreams do come true!

6.30.13

Right after the concert, we headed to the funeral of my high school friend. She sadly lost her battle. I was hesitant about taking my kids to a funeral just a month and a half after their dad's passing, but they were resilient and even prayed over my dear friend. Immediately after the funeral, we hit the wilderness trail for some time with nature.

My intentions for this trip were twofold. I wanted to overcome any fear or reservation of keeping traditions alive, and I wanted to spread some of John's ashes in the Delaware River. I knew he would give me a thumbs-up on both counts. We made beautiful memories on that river.

I thought this sojourn would be tough, given the memories we brought to it, but we happily settled into the same campsite we had gone to for nine years as a family of five, but we pitched our tent—well, Angel met us there and pitched our tent—in the exact spot John-Marlon claimed every year.

When it was time, I climbed into a raft for our three-hour trip, but the uninviting murky water distracted me immediately. It had rained pretty heavily the night before, and the result was not to my liking. It didn't sit well with me to spread John's ashes in this dirty river, and I struggled with whether to go ahead with my plan. A dilemma. I decided to go forward and bring the vial with his ashes.

Angel brought his fancy waterproof camera so he could record the moment we spread his ashes. Along the way, we decided to stop at some rocks to gather for a prayer.

We had no set plan for where we would stop along our route, but in a surreal way, we were all drawn to a spot none of us had paid much attention to before.

There was no exchange of words; we all pulled over instinctively. It was a waterfall, a small one, but still a waterfall. The area was packed with people taking pictures. We decided this was the place to fulfill one of my intentions. We would spread John-Marlon's ashes there.

We angled our rafts at the shore, and as we climbed over jagged, slippery rocks and tried to avoid some dangerous falls, we soon discovered that if we passed the waterfall, we would behold a mysterious tunnel. Here, the gushing water was so strong that we yelled over nature to let each other know to walk to the other side. I held my girls' hands tightly as we moved against the flow of water. We were forced to plant firm steps to avoid letting the water sweep us forward.

As we made our way slowly through the tunnel, I heard a big splash behind me. Angel had fallen hard, but his arm was extended up and high, protecting the vial with the ashes from so much as a drop. I smiled, and he looked perplexed.

I walked ahead carefully, noticing there were fewer and fewer people around us. As we emerged from the other side of the tunnel, the noise, the people, and the strong force of the river beneath our feet were gone. We were greeted by peace and quiet, alone in this magical paradise.

As we lifted our heads to appreciate this little piece of heaven, we were stunned by the presence of a butterfly that pranced over our heads. It clearly wanted us to take note of it, and I knew from the moment I saw it that this creature of God was going to bless us in some way.

It fluttered over us like a helicopter, and it seemed to watch our every move. I wanted badly to receive a sign from John-Marlon via the butterfly, but I convinced myself not to focus on a sign because I did not want to be disappointed.

At that moment, Angel broke the terrible news that his camera battery had died, and he no longer had enough power to record spreading John's ashes. I was crushed, but within seconds, I realized that perhaps this moment was not meant to be recorded. My recovery time was so quick that I don't believe Angel even noticed my initial disappointment.

As I tried to focus on the task at hand, I couldn't help but be aware of the butterfly still watching over us. It was blue and black, and it was one of the biggest butterflies I have seen. Almost in unison, we gathered in a circle, and were led in prayer by our friend Yohvanni. He had a sweet idea. He directed us to go around our circle and share one word to describe John-Marlon. "Incredible," "powerful," and "fun" bubbled up; mine was simply "peace." John-Marlon represented peace to me. Peace in his final days. And peace in his passing, as his peace was transplanted into my heart when he transitioned to heaven.

I took out the vial and handed each of my children some of their father's ashes. Angel surprised me by sticking out his hand as well, and before I knew it, all eleven people with us, including children, extended theirs for ashes. I was beyond touched.

When everyone had ashes, we joined hands—one piled on top of the other—and dropped the gray flakes carefully, watching them fall into crystal-clear water and then downstream. They would travel through the tunnel, down the waterfall, and straight into the Delaware River, just as I planned.

I cleared my tears and looked up, seeing exactly what I expected: The butterfly was eye to eye with all of us, except my son, Marken, who was perched on a rock. The butterfly had a purposeful flutter as it seemed to circle the group, looking for something very specific, and we soon discovered what it was.

The butterfly began to circle around Marken, first in front of his face, and then over his head, and then it rested on Marken's head for what seemed like a long minute. Before we could tell Marken what was happening since he couldn't see it, he said, "I feel it."

For the first time, I realized that Marken's smile reminded me of his dad's smile. We stood in complete awe and appreciation at this miracle of communication. We have to believe!

As we exited our quiet tunnel-paradise, the scene turned immediately into Grand Central Station. The crowd of onlookers had discovered our wonderland, too.

As we walked back in deep thought, our silence was broken by joyful laughter as Yohvanni started screaming, "Thank you, John! Thank you, John!"

Two days later, I was loading the last bit of gear into my car. I became emotional at the sight of the empty campsite that was once full of *his* presence. I took John-Marlon's urn and sat by myself, holding it and blasting "Gone, Gone, Gone" from my car. After a few minutes, my friend's twelve-year-old son said, "Excuse me. Can I join you?"

I looked up, crying inconsolably. "Of course. Please do," I muttered.

Within minutes, all of our friends gathered and joined in prayer for our once head-chief-of-fun.

When we were ready to depart from the campsite, a beautiful blue-and-black butterfly appeared, eerily similar to the one at the waterfall. This one circled, also with purpose, around our campsite; once everyone appreciated its presence, it disappeared as quickly as it arrived. We were all silent as we followed with our eyes; no one's lips formed a word.

7.5.13

Today I had an aha moment! For the last couple of weeks, I began to stress over the aftermath of John-Marlon's death: bills, mounds of paperwork, organizing, cleaning, dusting, having a garage sale, filing, emptying John-Marlon's closet, and thoughts of becoming a hoarder. You know the deal. In the last couple of days, I have had profound conversations with the people I trust most (you know who you are), and I had a moment of clarity.

For goodness' sake, I survived the death of my husband. Am I seriously worried about things that can be put on an Excel spreadsheet and dealt with by addressing them immediately, doing them later, or deleting them from my list altogether?

With John-Marlon gone, I have every excuse to become paralyzed, but I cannot waste precious time on insignificant things or thoughts.

7.8.13

When I started attending church sixteen months ago, I did so because I had hit rock bottom and was at the lowest point of my life. From the moment John-Marlon and I set foot inside, we knew something was different. The building had permanent letters etched on the concrete wall as we entered: *Jewish Center.* I had no clue what to make of this, but in that instance, I knew that this Christian church was super cool. I sensed that its mission was not necessarily strictly about organized religion, but of spirituality. There was some Joel Osteen stuff happening in my own backyard.

We were greeted with tremendous love and handed the bulletin for the service. We had coffee and snacks at our disposal and were escorted as new members to our seats. From the moment the service started, we knew this was our new home. We were urged, as first-time guests, not to participate in the offering. People were dressed casually, and as communion came by, I rejected it the first time. How could I accept communion when I had not confessed? I later found out I rejected a cracker and grape juice and there was no need to confess to take communion. There was actually no formal confession done at the church.

John-Marlon was so embarrassed that I shooed away the usher, as if I needed the entire church to take note that I was a sinner and wasn't worthy of a mundane Keebler cracker. This church was definitely special. The music and angelic voices reached straight into the deepest part of my soul and had me in tears. I almost always cry. The service is that deep! Oh yeah, and there is a slideshow with the words to the songs so I can interact and sing along. The karaoke singer in me thanks the Bridge Church.

This church transformed our lives in the most profound way. We both learned to surrender, and eventually, we were blessed with peace beyond understanding in our journey. Pastor Dan became great friends with John-Marlon and was even with him the eve before he passed. I recall him looking up at Pastor Dan, smiling. "I'm ready to be with Jesus," he said. Pastor Dan returned a gentle smile.

7.9.13

Love! So much precious time wasted because we just don't realize how precious our life is. In 2011, I dedicated *"El Amor Que Perdimos"* (The Love We Lost) to John-Marlon one too many times. Back then, it felt good to cry as I listened to it, and it brought me some sick comfort to know that this song would break his heart every time I sent it to his phone. I can share this without any emotion attached because the girl who dedicated the song was not yet a woman.

I grew up shortly after. He died knowing I never stopped loving him. He left me knowing that I was his soul mate and he was mine. Our relationship was pure magic, and very few people on this earth will experience the powerful connection we both had in what should have been a most tragic time. He said the lessons he learned while dying of cancer were worth dying for.

I get it, respect it, and accept it. I will never experience that kind of love again, and I am completely fine with that. Love with your soul, and never compromise respect or dignity. We hold back our love because we are in need of love. Seek a church, counseling, or a spiritual retreat to rekindle that love. Time wasted cannot be recovered. Life is only one.

To my beautiful husband, thank you for choosing me as your wife and allowing me to have a second chance at renewing my soul.

7.12.13

I have worn my hair in a bun since I was sixteen. My high school friends can vouch that the bun went from the top of my head to the back of my head. I only wore my hair free for weddings or big events and maybe another three random times any given year. This is the shortest I have ever gone, and the happiest I have ever been with my hair. I declare myself a girly girl! No more hiding behind my bun. Liberation.

7.13.13

I was interviewed in Spanish for a segment of *Too Blessed To Be Stressed*, which was hosted by a spiritual leader in his own right David Bisono. I spoke of John-Marlon and didn't cry, my Spanish flowed (Amen!), and I was empowered by the people I met in the waiting area.

"I had sight, but now have vision" was what spoke to my soul today. And, oh yeah, I am loving my hair. Cutting off my hair was critical to my growth. I not only feel empowered but I look like sheer power!

7.17.13

I am so proud that even through challenges, I have been able to care for my physical health and keep to my nutrition goals. Even though I slacked off on my workouts, the body is so miraculous. It's like riding a bike. It has a memory system. My body is showing me that it remembers how hard I have worked, and here come signs of my baby six pack! I am inspired every single day with the passion my husband left imprinted in my soul. Sunday's race will be as colorful as his life. I miss my husband dearly, but I cannot bring him back; I can make sure he is never forgotten.

7.21.13

In life, many will hug and support you when you are down, but some of those very people will not be your biggest supporters as you begin to rise from the rubble. It's important to remember that human beings are imperfect.

Let's keep in mind that we cannot please everyone all the time. When you begin to make others uncomfortable with your fabulousness, you are fulfilling God's unique purpose designed specifically for you.

When people don't celebrate your rise and try to suppress your greatness, that is their issue, not yours. We report to one person only on this earth, and he is truly the one that matters.

Make your Monday awesome, and if you make someone a little uncomfortable being fabulous, it's A-Okay.

7.22.13

How I wish I could turn back the clock and leave the house a mess, leave the bills piled, and live carefree—just be in the moment. I never met anyone who enjoyed life more than my husband. I don't say that because he is gone; I share that because it is true. Anyone and everyone who has ever crossed paths with him can vouch for that statement.

My husband never saw the adventurous side of me because I lived a life that was way too calculated. In my defense, I guess I had to in order to keep some type of structure in our lives. When I think of how far we have come, I cry, but I smile through the tears. I smile because I live in gratitude. The more gratitude I show toward my new life, the more God showers his blessings upon me.

7.23.13

Today, I took the kids back to the very hospital where their dad passed away. I could have chosen many different places for them to receive counseling, but I selected the very place they saw him last for many reasons. I don't want them to have a negative association with hospitals or any places that may remind them of their dad.

The kids had an excellent session, and the counselor confirmed that the children are doing well. Before we left, we stepped into the hospital chapel and prayed for their dad.

In the car, Natalia complained of growing pains (those legs keep growing), and Ava just became a loving pain to her big sister. As they began to tease and poke at each other in the back row, I decided to check in with my mom as I do every day. I dialed her from the car speakerphone. I had to yell for my mom to hear me as the girls became louder and louder. I also sensed some poking going one. Just as I was about to reprimand them, my mother's call dropped, and the radio blared "Gone, Gone, Gone."

The girls immediately stopped arguing. Complete silence engulfed us in the car, except for our anthem of hope. We began to sing at the top of our lungs, and as the song wound down, our voices became whispers as we sang the final line: *I'll love you long after you're gone, gone, gone.*

I quickly turned around to celebrate this most perfect timing, and my six-year-old Ava was crying quietly.

Natalia, my nine-year-old, said, "Ava, that was Dad telling us to stop arguing."

Before I could ask Ava why she was crying, I heard Natalia break down and sob uncontrollably. I looked over at Marken in the front row, and he was stoic.

What happened to our perfect counseling session where the kids were talking and chatting up a storm about their dad in such a hopeful manner? Life happened. No matter how much I manage to shed light in the midst of darkness, nothing can ever take away the pain of losing their dad.

It was the longest ride home. Ava yelled over and over and over, "I'm just a baby. Why did I have to lose my daddy?"

Natalia, usually the mother hen, also expressed that she had many questions she could not put into words. Marken was still stoic. As I drove home, tears streaming down my face, I encouraged the kids to continue to cry and let it all out. It was a tough night, but we will survive this and will be okay. I have faith.

7.25.13

I am enjoying this beautiful day in Miami. Yep, Miami. I decided to refuel on a girls' trip, and I don't feel guilty. I deserve this. I am getting my dancing shoes ready for tonight. Crowds used to circle around us to watch John-Marlon and I dance *bachata* and merengue. I miss my dance partner, but our memories will be etched in my heart and soul forever.

We all grieve in different ways: I grieve the way John-Marlon asked me to—to never forget what we had and to create new memories because I deserve to live. Before I go to sleep every night, I pray, and I thank John-Marlon for being so amazing to me. He is my light; he is still my life.

7.28.13

My flight was delayed by four hours, and I had a middle seat in a tight row. But as life would have it, I received the gift of a nice, roomy seat right at boarding. The seat should have gone to a guy standing in front of me in line, but what a gentlemen. He smiled when the gate attendant skipped him and gave it to me. Good karma never goes unrewarded; he also nailed an awesome seat.

Ninety minutes to go, but I am cozy! When life hands you lemons—or a bad seat on a plane—just chill out. Ask the universe for what you need, and more often than not, you will receive. A great attitude goes a long way.

7.29.13

After the strongest hugs from my kids this morning, I am enjoying the peace of my house. The quietness and the loneliness my heart feels are completely welcome. I am learning that crying is not a sign of weakness, but of cleansing. I actually feel empowered after a good cry. I cry in gratitude—if that makes any sense.

I recharged in Miami, but my heart can't help but miss what I can't have. I know everyone has a different view of death, but in my pain, I know in my heart that John-Marlon was only meant to live his short thirty-nine years. The person I am today would not have been possible without the lessons I learned through his illness. Please don't get me wrong: I hate cancer. However, the lessons John-Marlon and God taught me would not have been possible without his death.

Eight months ago, John-Marlon and I attempted to save his life by sending him to the Hippocrates Health Institute. I firmly believe that the holistic practices we adapted extended his life, but the cancer was too vicious to control. When he returned after his trip, it was magical to watch the hug between John-Marlon and the kids who loved him so very much. I have that moment embedded in my head, and I took a picture, knowing in my heart how much I would soon cherish it.

7.30.13

We argued when he bought himself a BMW—an M5 at that! In cleaning the garage *again*, I am running into memory after memory. Finding the M5 license plate actually made me smile. When I didn't speak to him for making this insane purchase, he said, "I think I'm going to die. Please let me enjoy life." And so I did.

He ended up selling the car just a few months later because he said people would want to race him on the highway, and he was too tempted to prove who was fastest. (Typical man?) In his final months, he apologized profusely for his lavish lifestyle while we had moderate incomes. He actually said the old him was a jerk, but in hindsight, I am glad he lived it up, and he wasn't a jerk. He was the purest person I have ever met.

In his final days, he preached to anyone who would listen that material commodities are superficial and do not bring happiness. He said money makes things easier, but it will never fill your soul. In the end, he gave many of his toys away, and he felt great in doing so. He smiled a big old smile when he was able to do so. The recipients felt uncomfortable accepting gifts from a dying man, but John-Marlon had the most amazing sense of humor. He said, "I'm not giving it you because I am dying. I am giving it to you because I want you to have it." His smile was contagious.

8.4.13

The *beep beep* of a car alarm just made me jump out of bed—and then disappointment set in, knowing it's not him. It's not his car, and he will not be walking through the door. Wow. The sharp pain in my heart. Sometimes my life seems surreal. Moments like this catch me off guard, yet I could never prepare for them. I am fine, though, just a little jolt to the system.

8.5.13

This weekend, I spontaneously joined members of my church for a retreat at Camp Taconic. I had limited phone reception—exactly what my family needed. My children received my undivided attention.

The weekend was dedicated to praising God and having fun; we also delved into overcoming personal fears. My biggest fear is drowning. I have the few swimming skills that John-Marlon taught me, but I refused to have him teach me any further because I was too afraid. I almost drowned when I was ten and never recovered from that nightmare. Camp Taconic required a swim test to swim in the deep end of the lake. Natalia and Marken passed easily and urged me to take the test. I didn't think I could pass, but they insisted that I try.

I jumped in and almost immediately started gasping for air, but I found the strength to proceed with the test. I didn't want to let down my children. The test consisted of swimming seventy-five yards—three-quarters of a football field—and tread water for one minute.

As I swam the last twenty-five yards, I wanted desperately to quit, but heard my kids cheering for me. Once I heard the lifeguard yell for me to start treading water, I panicked because I realized that I had never learned how to tread water. My only training was minutes before from my daughter and another ten-year-old. I came out of the lake defeated, even though I had given it my all.

I couldn't do it.

Hours later, and minutes before the waterside activities closed, I got the urge to try again. I wanted to do it for my husband. I wanted to show him how far I had come by being as adventurous with my children as he was and overcoming my darkest fear. I had already overcome my fear of the dark, and this would be another victory. Three amazing women prayed over me before I attempted one last time. The lifeguard also suggested that singing a favorite song in the water would distract me from my fear.

I walked up to the edge of the deck, stared at the water, and prayed. The lifeguard gave me some final tips as Ava said, "You can do it, Mommy."

The second lifeguard joked that I should imagine Shaun T yelling, "C'mon, y'all, let's go!" I had shared with him earlier how I was an Insanity fanatic.

I smiled awkwardly and took the plunge. The moment my head surfaced above water, I panicked. But then, just as quickly, I remembered to sing. I began to play "Gone, Gone, Gone" in my head. I could barely remember the words, but then they came to me.

I placed all my trust in God and in John-Marlon. As I made the last turn, I continued to sing the song in my head, but the presence of fear overtook me. As I struggled to keep my body moving, my mind began to engage in a battle of its own.

A voice in my head said, "You can't do this."

Before I could entertain the thought, the lifeguard yelled, "Tread water!"

This was it—do or die. I began to tread and could hear my kids, my friends, and the lifeguards cheering for me. My biggest worry was letting them all down.

I kept seeing one lifeguard look at the other lifeguard for a time check, and it was as if he was begging him to speed up the clock. I know he felt terrible as he could see the look of panic, desperation, and despair as I began to flail my arms and legs in a motion that could only indicate that I needed help! I was fighting to stay afloat, and I was just hoping not to drown.

The lifeguard kept yelling, "Hang in there!"

How could I quit? I was now taking in water, and I could no longer breathe. But then I heard cheers! I had completed the swim test. I was so weak that I could barely make it back to the ladder. I emerged to a flurry of hugs and high-fives, and I had earned my red bracelet.

We ended the evening by lighting a flying sky lantern in John-Marlon's name. As it flew up into the night sky among hundreds, maybe even thousands of stars, we yelled, "We love you, Dad!"

Living fearless is a big statement, but when you begin to conquer your fears one at a time, you don't change who are you are—you change *how* you are. I doubt I will ever jump into another lake to test my swimming abilities, but I will keep this experience in mind when fear makes its next debut.

8.6.13

On August 3, 2012, my daughter painted a beautiful piece in her art class: an adorable puppy. I was so impressed with her talent, but her dad was even more impressed. On August 5, I had a girls' day with Natalia and Ava since John-Marlon would be going "fishing" with Marken. But they did not go fishing. Instead, Dad and son conspired to drive to Massachusetts to the home of a breeder and buy a six-week-old puppy that looked eerily familiar to what Natalia drew.

When John-Marlon surprised the kids with this puppy as a reward for Natalia's lifelike artwork, the girls went crazy. I, on the other hand, whipped out my six-inch heels because I would die before having that puppy lick me. Yes, you guessed it: I'm also afraid of dogs. I nearly had a nervous breakdown (not kidding), and I received many calls from people asking if John-Marlon had lost his mind. How could I say no to a man fighting cancer? I overcame my fear, and Buddy is now my jogging pal.

Buddy became family, and once I knew that John-Marlon was going to leave us, I knew I could never give away the dog. Buddy was one of the last gifts my husband left for our children. As John-Marlon neared his final days, he begged me to give away the dog because he knew I was drowning with responsibilities—and the puppy was now eighty pounds and rambunctious. He ate everything and began to feel the sadness in our home, sensing the pain yet to come.

Ironically, John-Marlon began to resent the dog when my attention was split between them. Becoming a caregiver was taking its toll on my mental well-being, but family and friends began to come to the rescue by helping me care for and entertain our children. One of those friends was a beautiful high school friend. Erica took my kids several times, and on one of those occasions, Ava said, "Erica, I think you would make a good mommy to Buddy. Do you want him?"

I made the difficult decision to accept Erica's offer to take Buddy even if it turned out to be a temporary solution. I preferred to give away the dog while John-Marlon was alive. Now, I could care for John-Marlon exclusively without worrying about this overgrown pup. It was one of the hardest decisions to make, next to telling my children that their dad had passed and letting my husband know that he had days to live. When we dropped off Buddy and said our good-byes, my heart broke for my children and the lives we once had. We were a family of five with a dog, and here we were, four of us driving away, leaving behind this most precious gift.

Today, Buddy is doing very well in his new home with his new mommy and family. He has a stepsister by the name of Sienna, and they play and are quite silly all day long. My kids have visitation rights, and just like with their dad, the memories remain.

What dad replicates his daughter's painting with a real dog and drives six hours to find the perfect match? John-Marlon was one of a kind. When the children think of Buddy, they think of their dad. Memories live forever.

8.7.13

I just realized that the most important task for me to complete is to preserve John-Marlon's memory. I wanted to watch my wedding video and realized it's on a darn tape. I need help transferring videotapes into DVDs, scanning thousands of pictures, archiving pictures from my computer and phone, and getting organized so I can preserve memories. Organization! How I suck at it.

Friends, when taking pictures and video footage, remember to archive them in an organized way. You never know when those moments will be the only thing you have to hold on to.

8.7.13

Today, I took a few minutes to watch my wedding video, and I had a bit of an out-of-body experience. I looked at the beautiful girl in the video and couldn't help but want to rewind the clock and give that young girl some advice.

If I could—I would tell her to look deeper into her husband's beautiful eyes, to offer to drive on long trips, to laugh a little louder, to hug a little tighter, and fight a little wiser. To find a purpose that fulfilled *her* soul so that her husband can be an added blessing in her life but not *her everything*. I would tell this young girl to live her life as if she only had thirteen years of marriage with her soul mate. Yet, the clock never ticks backward—for a reason. Our experiences make us who we are.

Through God's grace, I was able to become the very woman who I hoped that girl could be. It took a tragedy to transform me from just living to living with purpose.

John-Marlon stared into death's face, and instead of fear, embraced it. He repeatedly told me that he was ready to go, and sometimes he said it with a big smile.

In his departure from my world, I can see so much more clearly now. If I had to give that young girl real life concrete advice on how to love, I would give her my recipe for love, with my five secret ingredients:

1. Accept his differences.
2. Make sure you have your own passion and your own dreams.
3. Respectfully agree to disagree.
4. When you agree to disagree, have enough compassion to meet on neutral ground.
5. Simply love him.

8.8.13

Yesterday marked three months since John-Marlon passed. I didn't even realize that until this morning. My post last night was fitting for the seventh of the month.

This morning, I would like to share an experience that keeps repeating itself. First and foremost, this post is not directed toward anyone specifically. This is about my personal experience.

It may be difficult for some to understand my grieving process; it may even make some uncomfortable. I don't glorify death, and I am not in denial. My heart breaks every single day. I make a conscious decision to be as strong as I am. I have been severely depressed before (when my life was "good"), and I don't wish that pain on anyone. And I don't wish to revisit it.

I have had people tell me to get off Facebook to take time for myself, to cry for days, to get angry, or to remember to grieve John-Marlon's death.

I was given a gift, and I choose to see it that way. The gift was temporary, but aren't we all on this earth? I was able to say good-bye. I was able to see the joy and peace in his heart. I was able to see him literally reach for heaven before he left the earth. I was even able to hold his hand for his final breath. I am in gratitude, and even through my pain and tears, I will remain as such because there were so many other ways this story could have ended. Yes, he will no longer be here for holidays or to help me raise our beautiful children. When I turn at night, I don't feel the warmth of my love, but instead a plush pillow. I recognize my pain because I live it.

I hope my posts come across as I intend. I intend to share my journey—not advise anyone how to grieve a death. Acceptance requires its own unique healing journey.

My post today is shared from a good place, and I completely understand the good intentions that are meant when people wonder if I am healing appropriately. Having a child with Asperger's has taught me that one size does not always fit all. Healing with gratitude fits me just right. John-Marlon wouldn't want it any other way. Trust me; he's watching.

God bless my Facebook family. You all play an important role in my life, giving me yet another reason to get up every day with new optimism. With every post comes another day of healing. With every comment and like you give me, John-Marlon's legacy lives on. Thank you.

8.9.13

Good morning, friends. Yesterday, I visited Natalia and Ava's summer camp for parent visiting day. I saw a mom taking a picture of her daughter, and I offered to take a picture of the two of them.

She said, "Oh no, I look awful today."

The moment she said that, I knew I would change the way she viewed the world in one minute flat. I told her about John-Marlon's passing and how I am presently scrambling to gather pictures, videos—just about anything so my kids can forever remember their dad. I showed her the picture I posted yesterday and told her how I couldn't stop staring at it because memories are all I have. Her eyes welled up, and so did mine. I walked away and left her thinking. I found her staring at me for the remainder of our visit, trying to lock eyes, to give me a warm smile, as she asked others to take pictures of her and her daughter.

My friends, I was blessed to say all the things that I didn't say in my marriage in his final months, but please don't wait for the perfect time to say those things that can fill your heart with love. Having pride is a terrible disease, but the beauty is that you hold the cure.

8.10.13

Sometimes, men show affection in ways that are alien to us. Sometimes, we expect them to guess how we need affection. So being that neither one in a couple is a mind reader, you can either share with him—in a loving way—what you need, or you can begin to realize that anything that seems like "an attempt" at being a good man is a score. So, pick your battles. I can't tell you how my every day is spent smiling at all of the small ways he used to love me. Hindsight is twenty-twenty. I would love to have a second chance, but that is not to be. At least not on earth. But do you? Smile.

How I wish you were here,
How I miss you, although you are near.
Now I know how you felt

When I was here,
But nowhere near.
I was always fussing and running around,
When you said, "Leave the cleaning and slow down."
I couldn't see what I had missed.
I now understand what I should teach,
I couldn't see what I had missed,
Until what I missed was not in reach.

8.11.13

Enjoying the last bit of summer and off to the Hamptons we go! There were no clean clothes, but I washed them and dumped them in a basket. Now we're good to go! Our clothes may be wrinkled, but they are clean.

I went to church this morning and had many new friends join me. I am so happy that my newfound faith is contagious. I want to give a special thanks to everyone who comments and inboxes me their own journeys as you learn from my lessons. There is nothing more in this world that I would love than to have my family back, but since it was not God's plan, I know that his purpose for me is to share my journey so others can find healing in their lives. Thank you for being so bold and letting me know that my life has influenced you. If you are a silent supporter, I am also grateful for you.

8.13.13

In my journey, I have learned the hard way that I can choose to look at a crisis as a breakdown or a breakthrough.

A breakdown means to "collapse, fall apart." Back in late 2010/ early 2011, I fell apart at a time when I should have been praising God for all of our blessings. I had a good, healthy husband, three healthy, beautiful children, the job of my dreams, and an elegant house in the suburbs. I somehow managed to be functional despite my severe undiagnosed depression. I was in such a dark place that I could barely stand the sight of my own face. I dreaded walking past mirrors. I even contemplated covering or removing all of the mirrors in my home, but I ultimately decided that was a stupid idea because I would also have to figure out how to dodge my reflection in public places too.

I tried to desperately rise from despair, but I lost my grip each and every time. I was losing the joy of living, and every time that John-Marlon tried to help me, my anger toward him grew furiously out of control. It was his fault I was miserable, or so I thought.

In 2012, when John-Marlon was diagnosed with cancer, I made a conscious decision to embrace this new crisis as a breakthrough—no matter what the outcome. A breakthrough as in "discovery." I opened my heart and began to understand that my journey was not only a discovery about me—it was about all the lessons that God intended me to learn along the way.

There is pain that is so unbearable that our souls scream for mercy. I have been there—and I know. However, I learned that when God puts my faith to the test, he is preparing me for his inevitable greatness. When the weight on your shoulders is too heavy to carry, always rely on God. Learn to surrender the things you cannot control. When you surrender, you are making a conscious decision to have a breakthrough and not a breakdown. A breakdown only happens when you resist accepting the very thing that is causing you pain. Surrender and exhale. Tomorrow is always a new day.

8.17.13

What a productive day! I slept over at my mom's house because I was super-emotional of my upcoming birthday. For the last fifteen years, John-Marlon has planned my birthday. My heart was so sad this morning, the saddest it had been in a while. Thank God for my girls; they keep me on my toes and don't give me a second to relax!

My sister mapped out my plans and projects for the remainder of the year, and my best friend took over my birthday plans because I am way too emotional to think. Last year, I complained to him (in front of everyone) about the surprise birthday party he organized for me in the midst of his illness. How selfish of me. I have grown, thank God, and recognize that, but it still brings me sadness to know I wasted so much time on not living in the moment.

I am grateful for my circle that reminds me I was an amazing wife. I tend to forget. In the end, loving is painless. Not loving enough is quite painful.

8.19.13

On this sweet morning, I dropped off the kids for bereavement camp at the hospital where John-Marlon passed away. I am grateful to live in a country where my kids can have a fun week while healing and facing head-on all of the emotions of such a profound loss.

They were all smiles and embarrassed that I kept hanging out to make sure they were comfortable. Tough kids.

Before I left, I visited the hospital chapel where I had prayed so hard for healing in John-Marlon's final days. Healing didn't happen on this earth, but John-Marlon was healed the moment he left us. John-Marlon and I were so afraid of death, but death lost its sting once we surrendered our fear of the unknown.

When someone you love dies, your senses become heightened. I find myself staring at the sky, appreciating the rain, listening to birds, watching butterflies, and looking out for the cardinal that visits us often. I now also know his scent. Yep, it only took fifteen years to figure that one out. He knew every detail about what I loved and disliked. He studied me like a map, and he tried to please me with anything my heart desired and then some. He's lucky I was a woman who held her own and who had no desire to be fulfilled by material things. Otherwise, yikes!

I married with the idea that my husband would always need to love me more than I loved him. I made every effort to drive that point home whenever I could. Talk about being arrogantly insecure.

Protecting your heart from being hurt is pretty silly when you think about it because your heart is already pretty damaged to begin with if that's your take on love. Love hard—or don't love at all. You will never experience the joy of loving if you don't love with your entire heart. Never.

I am so glad for the hundreds of kisses and hugs I gave to John-Marlon and the opportunity to look into those gorgeous green eyes and make peace with my mistakes as he did with his.

His scent is healing, and eternity is fitting for the place he holds in my heart now and forever.

8.20.13

Aw, my heart is so happy—and yes, I'm about to tell you why. Natalia, my nine year old walked into her first modeling interview and walked out fifteen minutes later with a contract from one of the top New York City modeling agencies.

When we walked in for her interview, I was so embarrassed when they asked me if I had her pictures or a portfolio. All I had was a photocopy of a random picture I took in her soccer uniform weeks earlier. I was so unprepared and wasn't thinking that morning. I thought I blew it, but fifteen minutes later, after the agency met her and had her read a script, I was handed a contract.

I don't know what the future holds, but I believe now more than ever that our destiny is already written. We just have to be obedient and trust that it will all work out. John-Marlon must be working hard in heaven, and I don't expect anything less from him.

8.20.13

Today, at camp, the kids watched a memorial video of all the loved ones they lost. Instead of glamming it up with sparkles, Ava requested a "tattoo" with the word *Dad* and a heart. When I picked her up, I could see in her face that the day had been emotionally draining. I held her so tightly for a good twenty minutes as she stared off in deep thought. I know she will be fine; she has proven to be the toughest little girl I know.

She had a school project at the end of the school year and noted that we are a family of five on her assignment.

A brat classmate—nah, I don't mean that, yeah I do—reminded her that her dad died, and she has only four people in her family.

Ava said, "We are five, and my dad lives in heaven!" Feeling is healing. I know my kids are getting stronger and stronger every day.

As I type and listen to music, I have a tender memory of John-Marlon. I decided to play Sarah McLachlan's "In the Arms of an Angel."

My son ran upstairs and said, "Mom, you need a hug. You are listening to one of the saddest songs in the world." He smirked and then ran away.

So much for my sad moment. I am smiling at how resilient he is, and I know that I can always rely on him for comic relief. I've been told he belongs cracking jokes on a stage. With an eleventh-grade reading level in seventh grade, he is going to be cracking books for a little while longer before he makes his debut.

I am blessed. Thank you, God, for my strength. Thank you, John-Marlon, for your continued light! Keep shining on us. I am eternally grateful for your undying love! I feel it.

8.22.13

Tonight, I had the kids create their own personalized memory boxes. I found myself gasping for air every time one of them mentioned a memory of their dad because it saddened me to think that they may forget their sweet memories as time passes. *Should I grab a camcorder, record it in my journal, or just leave it be?*

My brain has hurt for the last month while trying to figure out how to preserve his memory in a meaningful way. I want to remember every little bit of him, and I am saddened because I know some of it will escape me.

8.23.13

An empty driveway has brought me back to May 7, the day I lost John-Marlon, but it has also allowed me to relive beautiful memories.

As I saw his truck being towed away, I thought, *This truck has many camping stories to tell. It has been driven a tiny bit recklessly through the sand dunes on private beaches that only John-Marlon could have figured out existed. This truck was what I looked forward to seeing pull up every night.*

My heart always skipped a beat for him, but I didn't always show it because from the time the car pulled into the driveway to the time the door opened, my open heart unintentionally converted into the nagging wife.

From the moment I saw the tow truck, my heart sank. No, it didn't sink—it shattered. I cried a good cry as the driver maneuvered into position, unaware of my neighbor running toward me until she was by my side. She held me, and we cried together. The moment brought some healing.

I stared at the truck being driven away and carefully turn the corner just as I watched John-Marlon's hearse pull away and slowly take that final turn as if allowing me to savor every second of what once was the physical John-Marlon.

8.24.13

My birthday! Thank you all for the most amazing, beautiful, thoughtful, heartfelt messages. I am at Joe's Crab Shack, the same place, same table that we ate at on John-Marlon's birthday, March 11. He is with us in spirit! I am uplifted by the love on a day that I am without my true love. God bless you all.

I continue to read your beautiful messages, and I will read again when I am in the quiet of my own space. Thank you again. I am smiling at all the love! For me, today is bittersweet. I celebrate life and reflect on love. On the way home from lunch with my kids, we heard Bette Midler's "The Rose."

I have never listened to the words until today. I am now having an undisturbed moment as I appreciate the beautiful words Bette sings of love, but not through rose-colored glasses. Her words share the struggle and pain that sometimes arises as you both grow. However, if you love, nurture, and be patient, love will certainly blossom.

8.25.13

Thank you all again for the outpouring of birthday wishes. I have read each and every one. When someone is fragile, that is when she needs the most support and uplifting, and for that, there are not enough thank-yous to let you know how grateful I am.

To all my friends and family who made time to spend with me, I am eternally grateful. To me, the entire night was special, but I want to give a special shout-out to my old friend Rich for being my dance partner last night. As I threatened—I mean, nicely asked—Rich to make sure he left it all on the dance floor, he twirled me like a mad ballerina. Even though every twirl was faster than the last, the movements played out in slow motion in my head as I recalled the magical moments John-Marlon and I had as we captivated the "audience" who would watch us grace the dance floor. It was an emotional ending to an amazing night. My tears shed from a place of gratitude, knowing that my love for music and lyrics comes from the best teacher I ever had—my husband.

As I was getting dressed yesterday, I played a song on my computer (at least a dozen times) that many of you have tagged me in. As Marc Anthony's *"Vivir Mi Vida"* was playing on full blast, Ava ran up to me and said, "That was Dad's favorite song." I smiled because the dedication of this song on my Facebook wall over and over was no coincidence—it was a *Godincidence.*

I learned something new about my husband from my six-year-old. I look forward to discovering more about myself as I travel this road that has never been traveled because this is my life, my own unique journey, just as you have yours.

8.27.13

I have gone from a size ten to practically a size zero, and it didn't happen through suffering and starvation. I can't begin to tell you how many people think my weight loss is from depression. I used to explain but now I just nod in agreement. We move away faster from that conversation if I handle it that way.

I share my size because so many women have asked me how I went from a ten to a zero in a matter of five months, and how I maintain it. I lost the weight at a time when I was dealing with severe depression, a husband facing terminal cancer, fighting a legal battle with the school district, and working eleven hours a day. I started working out so I wouldn't lose my mind completely.

If I could share any advice with women who are secretly running on empty, feeling fat, or overwhelmed, it is to stop! Stop putting yourself second. We want to do everything and be everything to everyone, but we are left depleted, and in my case, even resentful. There is nothing more fulfilling than doing for others, but not when it affects our ability to live a purposeful life. You must be consistent if you are to get the most from your faith, good nutrition, your fitness, your career, or life in general. Make a choice to make a change, and commit. If you don't know where to start, nutrition is where it's at. I have one word for you: alkaline.

9.2.13

John-Marlon fulfilled his purpose on this earth in his short thirty-nine years. The lessons I have learned would have never been possible without his passing. In the silence, in my pain, in the emptiness is where I learn the most valuable lessons. The lessons cannot be learned unless I accept that my husband's passing was timed and written way before he was born. God called him home. This by no means is easy to swallow, but once I began to accept this as fact, my healing began to take shape. To accept God's plan means that you can move on with your life without bitterness, without anger, without regrets. Sadness is always in my heart, but I always make it a point to water it with the joy of beautiful memories.

I have made a conscious decision not to mourn his death; instead, I celebrate his life. There are no accolades for how much or how I long I suffer, and although grieving is different for each and every person, I choose to grieve with praise even through the pain because I was able to cross paths with him here on this earth.

Sharing our story has provided tremendous healing to keep his memory alive and to possibly touch a life that may need that spark of hope when the pain is too much to bear or the road is not easy to find.

9.4.13

For the last four years, until a few months prior to his death, John-Marlon had the morning shift with the kids. He would get up at six, shower, and beautify himself because he took great pride in his appearance. That man cared about his looks more than any man I have ever met!

Around seven, he would wake up the kids with a nice warm breakfast made with love. He had an amazing gift for cooking. He would then pack lunches and snacks, and help the girls get dressed when they were "too sleepy" to do it themselves. After teeth were brushed, he would tackle what no man should ever have to do: comb and style curly, unruly hair!

He mastered detangling with his trusty detangling spray and learned to comb out hair in sections. He would come up with the most creative hairstyles. Some worked, and on rare occasions, some just didn't quite cut it, but the girls were always happy.

Teachers and moms at school were constantly complimenting the girls' outfits and style. I take no credit for that. John-Marlon did the shopping for the kids as well. He knew when all of the Macy's sales were, so much so that two weeks before he passed, he told me to run to Macy's for their one-day designer pillow sale. He urged me not to take more than an hour because he had lost his ability to walk on his own and was afraid he might have to use the bathroom in my absence. I thought he was crazy, but he demanded that I go because this sale was worth it. I came back with fourteen designer pillows for eighty dollars. I have one body pillow that he used in those final days, and it brings me so much comfort and warmth at night. I know I steered off the school topic, but I have so many memories.

I miss him! Today was hard. Getting the girls ready made me a little teary eyed because I never said thank you for that morning shift. Not all dads can pull that off.

In life, I thought he was a good dad; after his death, I know he was an exceptional father!

Thought for tonight: Have an attitude of gratitude! Don't think it. Say it!

9.6.13

Today marks four months since John-Marlon left us. I can't say that sadness is what I feel. It's more like a terrible, terrible void in my heart that will never be filled. And I don't want it to be.

Would you believe that I miss him yelling at me for secretly using his expensive razor blades, for borrowing his boxers as my most comfy pajamas, and for using pots and pans that were clearly labeled "do not touch"? I was notorious for burning cookware before things were even cooked.

He was the most giving person I have ever met. He would buy me anything I needed or wanted, but touching his stuff was a big no-no! I, of course, never cared or listened to him. The friendly feud we had over the years was just part of who we were as a couple. Sometimes, he would just have to laugh and ask if I will be like this when I'm sixty! Little did we know that we would never see sixty together, at least not on earth.

Tonight I am having a little vino as I take in the realness of it all and stare into the biggest closet in my house. I haven't emptied his things yet. When I look at this space, I am not sure what I feel, but I do know that when the time is right, we will go through the items together as a family.

I won't remind my children of the significance of today. It's not a marker for celebrating, and it most definitely is not one for grieving. I am comforted to know that the man who lived one of the most adventurous lives in health told me in his final months that he was the happiest man on earth even though he no longer resembled his former physical self. Indeed, his smile never changed, and his eyes still sparkled, even when he said, "If God needs me, I'm ready."

And, as I get ready to head to my bed this early morning, I say, "I'm ready to serve God. What do you need from me?"

9.9.13

Good morning, all! Today starts a new chapter in my life. I will no longer squeeze myself into my own schedule. I am the priority in my schedule. It's just past seven, and I have worked out, meditated, showered, and am now sipping green tea (with my feet up), enjoying the magnificent trees in my yard. I don't think I have ever really looked at them.

I live with an attitude of gratitude, but I suffer from the same issues as everyone else. I get overwhelmed too.

After an amazing service at church yesterday, I realized if I survived the death of my husband, what the heck am I getting stressed over? Most of the things we worry about have already happened, and we cannot control them; the other chunk of worrying comes from things that will never happen. The worries that cripple us on a daily basis are miscellaneous issues that should have zero power over us.

I am a new person every day, and so are you. Anxiety is crippling even in small doses. I began to feel it creeping up on me, but I will not allow anything to get in the way of my peace.

From here forward, my mornings will feel and look just as they did this morning. Tranquil!

It's 7:30 a.m.—time to wake up my kids with the warmth and peace I feel in my heart. I will not to be the frantic mother who throws her excited, nervous energy onto her children. They are a reflection of me. Therefore, I am responsible for the joy and peace that surrounds our blessed home. I know I will slip up, but accountability is half the battle.

Have an amazing day.

9.11.13

Until two weeks ago, I thought humility was a bad word. At church last week, my pastor called me to the stage to speak of my joy in the face of crisis. This particular week, I was so happy to be in the audience listening to someone else's testimony. The person called to speak was someone John-Marlon greatly admired. The gentleman who was speaking served me communion every Sunday. He also attended the same Bible study that John-Marlon attended. To my surprise as he spoke on stage this day, I discovered he was also the creative director for the NFL, the brains behind the designs of everything NFL.

John-Marlon was a diehard football fan, and I find it completely God's work that he placed this powerhouse executive in John-Marlon's life—not to chitchat about football or to be impressed over extraordinary job but for the purpose of bonding as brothers in Christ. All of the men in the Bible study were witnesses to John-Marlon being his true self. He was able to read aloud in a Bible study. He knew that he would stumble, fall, and get stuck, but in God's home, we are all equal.

C. S. Lewis said, "True humility is not thinking less of yourself, but thinking of yourself less."

9.11.13

I haven't watched the news or TV in the last couple of days since I have been trying to lead by example. In skimming through the news, however, I now realize what today means. I just wrote a post about "ultimate humility," and twelve years ago, so many experienced "ultimate humility" as they risked their lives to save and comfort others. These were the unsung heroes—in and out of uniform.

Today is indeed a time to reflect on those lives lost, but let's remember that we don't have to relive it by watching the acts of horror on the news over and over. How about we each complete one act of kindness today in their collective honor?

9.12.13

I head back to work on Monday, and I'm thinking about what to wear on my first day. My T25 workout shirt and tutu skirt? I'm not sure if my six-inch heels complement the outfit. Well, of course I am kidding, but I can actually wear this outfit because as of Monday, I return to work—in a work-at-home situation.

I lost my husband, but I have gained many blessings. My latest blessing comes in the form of the fact that I can now do my job at home. To me, this is just another confirmation that my angel in heaven is hard at work. The greatest gift I have attained since his departure is my inner peace. I have worked hard to gain my peace, and after an extremely difficult day dealing with frustrating matters, I have proved that my inner peace is solid as a rock!

In addition to returning to work, I will be working hard at piecing my book together so I can have a book proposal ready by December 31 (my self-imposed deadline).

I love you all and hope my journey has inspired you in the slightest way. If it did, it means my husband's legacy lives on. That is enough for me when I lie down at night without him by my side.

God bless you for helping me through the most difficult time of my life.

9.13.13

I was organizing my basement (storage) closet, and I found my wedding dress! I held it so tightly and then got the strength to show my girls. They loved it. It's timeless. I had it in a plastic bag for thirteen years (don't judge), but it's as white and as pretty as when I bought it from the first wedding shop I walked into. It was also the only dress I tried on. We are preparing for a small garage sale tomorrow, and the kids are helping me organize it. They want me to try it on. Wish me luck. This is going to be so tough for me. My heart is pounding, but it is not the same pounding I felt when I first tried it on thirteen years ago.

9.15.13

Breaking Bad is breaking my heart! Well, it is not quite breaking my heart, but it is making me reflect, big-time. The show was one of John-Marlon's favorites, and he begged me to watch it with him. After five minutes, I decided it wasn't for me and returned to Facebook. Watching TV with your spouse may seem insignificant, and some of us ladies may prefer to use that time to bond and talk about feelings, but as I am about to go to sleep, I promise you that those moments are just as precious.

9.16.13

Time heals all wounds. This is not true. I used to say it all the time, but it's actually the worst sentiment to express to someone who has experienced loss. It gets harder in truth, but when you have a solid foundation, God will see you through in a big way.

I have had an interesting last couple of days as a single mom. I had to fiddle with a fridge that wouldn't cool, and I somehow fixed it. I had to go on a hunt to find the circuit breaker and began to label every switch. I cared for one bleeding daughter, while I consoled the other as she screamed, "Please don't die!" I have an outstanding support system, but there is nothing that compares to having one person who is your everything. I am now my own everything, and my new life is not easy.

My strength and clarity during this time comes from church, working out, and good nutrition. I have also incorporated meditation into my life. Meditation is my newest addiction, and I wonder how I ever lived without it.

9.17.13

It is spa time at the Suaza house! I have six TVs in this house, but only one is connected so the kids can watch for thirty minutes a day on school nights. That could potentially change, but I need to have more family bonding time at this juncture. Prior to my current structured schedule, they probably watched a few hours a day, but I made a conscious decision to interact more with my kids.

I always used to joke with John-Marlon that no matter how good we were to our kids, someone would end up in therapy, complaining about how we didn't love enough. I probably felt that way because we were raising them as consumers of the latest and greatest of everything and pacifying them with *things* instead of pure, simple love. We, of course, showered our kids with affection, but we were inadvertently teaching them that love is found mainly in things.

We live in a society where more is just not enough, and kids grow up to be adults who worship things. This isn't because they are materialistic, but it is the only way to continuously fill the void that can only temporarily be filled with tangible items.

When you don't know what it means to genuinely love yourself, you will forever walk around with a gaping hole in your heart.

9.19.13

I often joke that Carol was the third wheel in my marriage, but she truly was the glue that kept us together during many of our difficult years. Every time I would approach John-Marlon with empty divorce threats, I would run to Carol. She would console me in a way that few would dare. She would remind me that I was the problem—and not him.

"He hasn't changed," she said. "You have!"

She was right. I had lost myself in motherhood, and I completely forgot how to be a wife, how to have fun, and how to smile!

She would always say, "Don't divorce him. I'm telling you that it's a jungle out here. There is no one out here." She meant that good men were hard to find. John-Marlon was a good man, but my focus was off because I was looking to fix him instead of looking to accept him.

I have learned so many lessons from my younger friend. For one, I learned that happiness is a choice. Having lost both parents by the age of seventeen and being pregnant at that tender age, I never saw her break, but I always saw her smile. She was strong and optimistic.

In my twenties, when I compared my life to others and would wish for my life to be different, she would remind me that envying someone else's life means wanting every single bit of that life—not just the part of the life that you want to have. It only took one time for her to say that to realize that my life was just fine. Thank you very much!

My mom used to say, "*Dime con quien andas y te dire quien eres.*" Translation: "Tell me who your friends are, and I will tell you who you are."

9.22.13

Pastor Rick Warren eloquently said, "We don't ever get over grief; we get through it." With every passing day, I can understand my grief a little better. I am sad, and a little piece of my heart is sad every single day, but I can recognize that sadness is the emotion. I don't have to allow the other emotions that can come with sadness to paralyze my joy. I don't have anger, resentment, or regret, which are the very feelings that will deny me the opportunity to rejoice in John-Marlon's life.

When you can recognize your struggle, know that you cannot change it, and stop controlling the uncontrollable, you have surrendered to God's will—and that is liberating.

9.23.13

If I could disengage from toxic people in my life with the push of a button, would I do it? The answer is yes, and I have. With pushing that button comes the potential of losing friends and creating distance between family members, but life's purpose cannot be fulfilled with gossip, heaviness, complaining with no desire for a solution, and those who betray while patting your back. For me, there is no time to fix others when I am trying to find my own inner peace.

To disentangle or disengage does not necessarily mean cutting people out of your life, but it does create a nice space for breathing that feels lonely at times because you are no longer entertaining mindless chatter.

That extra time to reflect on who you are and what you stand and don't stand for may feel uncomfortable because you will be forced to look in the mirror and work on you! In an era where everyone wants to live happier, growing pains are not just for the young anymore.

9.24.13

Everyone has faith until faith is rocked to the core. Not until life smacked me in the face—and I mean hard—did I truly know where my relationship with faith stood. On the day I suspected John-Marlon had cancer, my faith disintegrated. I locked myself in a friend's bathroom and screamed without any regard that the midnight bell had just struck, bringing in the New Year of 2012.

As I made the conscious decision to build my relationship with faith, I faced the five hardest days of my life, trusting that God would see me through, and he did.

1. Telling my kids—ages five, nine, and twelve—that their father was going to die

2. Letting my husband know that it was okay to stop fighting—that we would meet again on the other side

3. Watching my husband's labored breathing as I awaited that final breath

4. Breaking the news to my kids that their dad had passed away

5. The day of his funeral

Having a relationship with faith is always best when things are going pretty well in life. Life can change in an instant, and getting caught off guard without a net beneath you can be quite painful.

My relationship with faith is not perfect, and it needs a tune-up more often than not (that's why I go to church), but it never fails to get me through the darkest moments. It is also present during precious, beautiful moments.

Faith is my antidepressant, but unlike a pill, you can't just pop one when you need it. Faith cannot be seen, it cannot be touched, and it cannot be measured. It is the conviction that no matter what the outcome, you will be okay. You will be okay!

10.1.13

When your inner peace is dependent upon someone else or your circumstances, you may need perspective on your life. We may question God's plan, but always lean on him to reclaim our peace. Know that his plan is not meant to break us down, but it will allow us to break through!

When things kept getting worse in my life, I thought, *It can't get worse than this.* Guess what? It can—and it will—because I kept telling the universe what I did not want!

On May 7, when I gave one final kiss to my husband as they prepared to wheel his lifeless body away, I never imagined I would walk out of Calvary Hospital and look up at the sky and appreciate its beauty, take a picture, and thank God. Since that day, I have enjoyed abundant blessings.

In my husband's death, I learned what it means to live! Therefore, he lives in me. Don't let a tragedy, a circumstance, or even a day take your inner peace and joy. Acknowledge the pain, and move forward in faith—even if you do it slowly.

10.2.13

I literally have chills running up and down my arms. Some friends gave me a book of inspirational quotes after John-Marlon's passing. I completely forgot about the book, but when I saw it today, I opened it to a random page. Without giving it any thought, I read the passage and was in awe of how it spoke to my soul. I smiled, but before I could walk away, I noticed the date—March 11! That is John-Marlon's birthday—another affirmation that my husband has never left my side.

Look for signs of your loved ones who are gone. They send you messages in ways that you will miss if you don't live in the moment. My heart is soaring, like when you have a crush on someone. I still have a crush on my husband even though we have a long-distance relationship!

> Walk by faith, not by sight. As you take steps of faith, depending on me, I will show you how much I can do for you. If you live your life too safely, you will never know the thrill of seeing me work through you. When I gave you my Spirit, I empowered you to live beyond your natural ability and strength. That's why it is so wrong to measure your energy level against the challenges ahead of you. The issue is not your strength but mine, which is limitless. By walking close to me, you can accomplish my purposes in my strength. (1 Corinthians 5:7, NKJV) Galatians 5:25

10.4.13

I am in Boston at a FranklinCovey training so that I can learn to manage my life better. Kindness is rewarded with kindness! We couldn't get into our room after two failed attempts with our room key. The security guard appreciated our no-problem attitude and brought us free breakfast vouchers and sparkling water. Cheers to spreading beautiful energy. I am loving Boston!

10.7.13

Good morning, all. Today marks five months since John-Marlon left this earth. Yesterday, Ava requested that she and her siblings write something in their memory boxes about Dad. It's as if she sensed what today is—even though I don't remind them of his monthly anniversary.

Ava remembers Dad having a date with her and enjoying Adventureland all by themselves. Marken remembers Dad being a little too adventurous and floating together down the Delaware River (wearing lifejackets, of course) without a raft. (I just found this out, by the way.) Natalia shared that when she puts on her smock in art class (Dad's old shirt), she can smell his cologne, and it makes her think of him. Eternity was his cologne, and we will think of him for an eternity.

My memory this morning is when I would wake up to him staring at me. I would laugh and say, "What are you looking at?"

He would smile confidently, touch my head, and say, "You!"

I never knew how powerful those moments would be until I could no longer have them. I miss him so very much.

I have a skylight in my room, and I talk to John-Marlon every night before I go to sleep. Although I cannot see him or feel his touch, I feel his presence just as I felt it when he stared at me at night. I feel the energy that flows around me, especially when I am in bed, and I know he continues to watch over me just as he did when he was right by my side.

10.7.13

In our thirteen years of marriage, we lived fifty! We loved each other from the moment our eyes locked, but we teetered on divorce many times and recovered while he was still in perfect health to be in love, in lust, inseparable, and in each other's souls. Love is forgiving. Love is unconditional. Love is free. Love does not have pride. Love is expressed in the eyes, in gentle touches, in flirty glances, in committing your hearts to the Lord, in late-night conversations with the TV off, and in long kisses. Sometimes love exists when you let go.

To hold hands, look into each other's eyes, and smile as the tears came—making a decision to surrender to God's will—is love. No more blood transfusions that were no longer having any affect, and no more being poked and probed without a cure in sight.

Love is hanging out in a hospital room, knowing that death is on its way, but still enjoying a basketball game together, sipping white zinfandel, cracking jokes all night, staring into each other's eyes, and knowing what each of us was thinking. Locking in an embrace on that final night, our souls became one and agreed to meet on the other side.

Love never dies!

10.8.13

Choice: The act of selecting or making a decision when faced with two or more possibilities—like "the choice between good and evil."

Even when a decision is not based on good and evil, the impact of not making a decision can make your soul and heart feel as if they were at war. Choices can be difficult, but not making one can have a much greater impact on your inner peace. For example, if you are overweight and choose not to make a choice to change, you are choosing to live in that zone of discomfort. It will always nag you until you surrender in defeat or claim victory over it. The same goes for the love we pour into our marriages, the bonds we create with our children, and the company we keep. There are certainly things that we have zero control over, and that is when we surrender to God.

What is tugging at your heart today? What is trapping your soul and leaving you unfulfilled? Really think about it, and begin to form an action plan. When you make a choice, you are holding yourself accountable for that decision—good, bad, or ugly. Many of us don't make choices because we don't want to be held responsible for making a wrong one. Fear is paralyzing.

I had to make three difficult choices. In making these decisions, I looked up for guidance and support, and I moved forward in faith:

1. *To place John-Marlon in hospice for the final week of his life so that we could bond as a family with support 24/7.* Doctors had given up hope months before, but we went into hospice, surrendering to God's will as we prayed for healing. His will was to take his son. God took his life, but he rewarded us with a peaceful death. He took his final breath with a beautiful exhale that I could hear and feel. I was blessed to watch the miracle of him leaving earth to go home.

2. *Cremating John-Marlon.* We decided as a couple that we did not want our children grieving over a grave. We recognized that his spirit will not live six feet under; it will be with us wherever we are.

3. *For me to celebrate life.* The act of him letting me know that it was okay to live after his death is an act of selflessness. The act of me obeying is also selfless. It is much easier to fall into depression and inner turmoil. I have been there—I know!

Choices are liberating! Make one today, but have peace in your heart in knowing that the outcome is not always in your control. Have faith in knowing that God knows the way.

10.10.13

The great escape! Today I decided to surprise my girls and sneak them out of school early. I felt bad lying, so on the early dismissal sheet, I wrote "appointment with mom"—not even a white lie—that's the truth.

As I waited by the main office door, I could see their confused faces as they made their way down the school hall. The girls were so happy. I told them that Dad asked me not to be a boring parent after he passed. I have to do silly things, and pulling them out of school is totally silly. He was the "fun" parent and worried I would live by rules every second of my life. I like rules, but rules are meant to be broken sometimes, and I can live with that.

10.11.13

The importance of a will, life insurance, and written final wishes should not be underestimated. These issues should be tackled *in life* so that our loved ones are not left with unanswered questions. I am guilty of not having all my stuff together, but this post is a reminder. Taking care of these issues is critical to your mental health.

Another reminder: If a loved one should pass, nothing gets you by like a good sense of humor, or not taking life so seriously. I could get stressed with these calls—but instead I had a little chuckle after I hung up. Check it out:

> Bill Collector: We know Mr. Suaza passed away, but there is still an outstanding balance on his business liability insurance.

Me: As I explained the last three times you called, you should have stopped charging the account five months ago when I shared with the company that he was critically ill and the policy should be terminated.

Bill Collector: Yes, but we never received anything in writing.

Me: Because he passed away.

Bill Collector: Yes, but we need something in writing to cancel the account.

Me: The corporation was solely under his name. I am not legally responsible for the business, so I ask that this be the last call I receive.

Bill Collector: Then we will have to send Mr. Suaza's account to collections.

Me: Knock yourself out.

10.15.13

Hi, everyone! I missed you. I took this weekend to disconnect from Facebook and spend serious quality time with friends and family in the mountains of Pennsylvania. We are all so entrapped in the social media world that we forget that sitting at a dinner table with family does not include going through a Facebook news feed simultaneously. For those of us with children, they are watching us, and we are setting the example of what is their norm.

A few months before John-Marlon passed away, he said something that completely changed the way I view and handle social media. It was heartbreaking and enlightening. During his final months, I was with him 24/7 (I was blessed to take a leave of absence from work). At times, I thought that lying next to him while reading Facebook news feeds was still being present because I was physically with him. I didn't realize how bad my addiction to social media was until he looked at me and shared his darkest fear.

Although I thought I knew everything about my husband and his condition, John-Marlon hid from me that he had Stage IV cancer for months. On one occasion when I was on my Facebook escape from the reality of my life, he looked at me and asked me to put my phone away. He said, "When I die, you can get on Facebook all you want."

My heart sank, but for a second, I thought that was a pretty mean comment. When I saw his eyes, I realized there was much more to his statement. I started going through papers like a madwoman as my gut told me to search—and there it was in print—stage IV cancer.

He was so strong physically and mentally that I never imagined that the cancer had spread. He wanted to protect me from knowing the inevitable, but he had to give me a warning that his time was limited. He did it in a way that truly made me take action. I checked out of Facebook for good to focus on my family.

Here are my social media takeaways when it comes to interfering with family time:

1. Never mix Facebook and family time (especially at the dinner table or in bed with your spouse).

2. Schedule a time when you browse through social media. Thirty minutes a day? Figure out what works for you!

3. Be the news—don't read all the news. Post things to inspire and motivate others. This will do wonders for your own soul. Don't be a slave to everyone else's reality, which for the most part, is distorted because you can only glimpse into their worlds.

4. If your priorities—children, significant others, parents, or friends—are not scheduled on your calendar, then they are not being treated as priorities. Schedule time—and keep those appointments just as you would with a business meeting or your social media time.

10.17.13

I cried a little, laughed a little, and did a whole lot of healing as I connected with two friends tonight. Friends are the family we choose. My kids are at my aunt's house, and I'm picking them up now. We are breaking all the rules tonight since bedtime will be midnight. But tonight was so worth it. I feel inspired, refreshed, and loved! I am blessed.

Are you living in the present? By no means is living in the present easy, but it is also not impossible. Your decision to live in the here and now will define your past, present, and future.

By choosing not to see what is right in front of you in the here and now, you lose the gift of the present because the present quickly becomes your past, and your past shows up in disguise and will call it "your future." The past will whisper lies, and you will believe every single one of them if you are not present.

You can easily be convinced—even brainwashed—into believing that you cannot change your circumstances, that you have "bad luck," or that you are not worthy. All of those things are lies. The lies are the equivalent to the fear that is placed in your heart by the enemy. You can call the enemy whomever or whatever you want, but in reality, the biggest enemy against you is you!

◎ Give thanks for what you have.

◎ Surrender to God those things you cannot control.

◎ Take a deep breath when worry overtakes your mind with trivial things, and ever so slowly, exhale; rinse and repeat as needed.

Living in the present moment requires nothing, but it can change everything. Living in the moment sometimes means smiling through the pain when you know you are having your last meal out as a family (just as we did) because you are grateful to have that very moment which in an instant will become your past, and define how you will embrace your future.

10.20.13

I told Ava that she can sleep with me tonight. I asked her to say her prayers, and this is how it went.

> Thank you, God, for food, for my home, for my school, for all of my family, and especially for my mom and dad. I wouldn't be happy if it weren't for all their love. Amen.

What a special little girl I have. She is so resilient and in faith. Blessed! Thank you, God, for our continued strength. Thank you, John-Marlon, for allowing our kids to feel your presence despite your distance. May God continue to bless you and bless us.

10.28.13

It may be quite difficult to believe that our personal trials are actually a blessing, but it may be even more absurd to believe that our pain is actually someone else's blessing—but it's true!

When Hurricane Sandy hit, John-Marlon was at the Hippocrates Health Institute in Florida. It was his last hope of surviving the fierce, monstrous cancer that had come with a clearly defined purpose: to take his life quickly and viciously.

I was left alone to fend for our children on all levels. Everyone was afraid of what was to come and preoccupied with their own safety. Although we were not entirely forgotten, I did not want to burden anyone with worrying about us. I knew our neighborhood was expected to be in the eye of the storm, but a tremendous peace prevailed over me. I knew that God would bless us, but I did not know how much. When God showed me his power in physical form on the evening of the storm, my undying faith was born. I will share that in tomorrow's post. I still get chills.

The aftermath of Sandy brought unprecedented devastation, but in that devastation, the good within all of us was nurtured. My church called members to action by asking us to find people who were affected by the storm—friends, family, or strangers. We were asked to choose a family to help, but our family couldn't help but to ask for an exception so we could bless two families.

Two of our friends experienced significant damage to their homes, but their circumstances allowed them to see how blessed they truly were. In their devastation, my family was provided a blessing in being able to partake in God's work by visiting their homes and presenting them with a small token of support—in the form of a check—on behalf of the church.

Ironically, a few months later, my pain would become their blessing because we were able to leave a small impression on their lives.

10.29.13

As Hurricane Sandy made landfall, I felt tremendous love from people around me. But when I shut my door, I was alone with my children. John-Marlon was still at the healing center in Florida. Flashlights on our heads, we hunkered down in the basement and prayed.

After the storm, there was an eerie calm. I stepped outside and captured on video the sea of darkness. There was one beacon of light that shone for miles—and it came from our home! This miracle enabled us to take in a family of five, and their dog, for one week.

My entire street, neighborhood, and community went black, but my home was shining brightly! I am certain that God chose me on that day to experience this small miracle because he knew I was ready to receive his glory. This was the day my faith was born.

Worrying will never change the outcome, and if you believe the universe's energy feels your vibrations, then the outcome will most likely not be what you want. Faith is a muscle I am learning to flex every day, and the beauty is that there will always be room for growth.

No matter what you are experiencing at this very moment, if God brought you to it, he will see you through it. Stay in faith, and watch small miracles begin to take form.

11.7.13

Today marks six months since John-Marlon passed. I truly cannot believe how quickly time has gone. Does it get easier? Not at all. I can't change what has happened, but I do have a choice. I can choose how to react to losing my husband, the father of my children, my soul mate.

My suffering will not change the outcome, especially since he is already gone. Finding joy in tremendous pain is an art form, a delicate and complicated dance, a gift that is God-given when you learn to surrender your pain to him. My resiliency actually comes from a place of compassion; by surrendering that which I cannot control, I maintain an inner peace within me, for my children, and in honor of John-Marlon's legacy. His smile, and his love for us and for life, will always be engraved in our souls. He is gone but never forgotten. His spirit lives.

To my husband, please don't ever forget that you are still our protector, and continue to guide our children toward healing every day of their lives.

11.12.13

As I drink green tea and stare out my window, I realize that snow is calming. It reminds me that the holidays are around the corner. Many emotions are being stirred now, but I have learned to tame them to work for me. The moment I begin to get anxious, I step back and realize that I have simply said yes too often. Learning how to say, "I can't" or "I am unavailable" or "I have too much on my plate" or "I'll try," including promises I make to myself, is darn hard, but it is sometimes necessary.

This is quite challenging because I have always been a people-pleaser. During my first holiday season without my husband, I realize that my inner peace trumps all. Even if I let others down by not being able to follow through, I give myself a pass. I forgive myself because I have never traveled this road, and I have never put my mental health first. My constant people-pleasing actions and carrying the world's weight on my shoulders led me into a vortex of chaos. When I pleased everyone, I failed myself. Failing myself is no way to please everyone.

11.15.13

A few weeks ago, I said I was about to make the boldest move I have ever made—and I did.

I purchased a vacation home for our family in the beautiful Pocono Mountains. I thought seriously before sharing this publicly because I didn't want people to imagine that I had lost my mind. Well, after I had that paralyzing thought about being judged, I snapped out of it and realized that I am worried about "the people." Who are the people? They don't really exist. If we really stop to think about it, we are worried about the imaginary, nonexistent masses that take hold of our minds and our lives. We have one boss to report to, and he lives upstairs. Once I realized that God was cool with my decision, so was I.

Out of three thousand homes in a private community, my future home was the only property that was up for sale with a beautiful creek flowing in the forested backyard. I know John-Marlon had a little something to do with it.

I envision doing a great deal of writing here and creating precious memories with my children as we learn to master skiing and snowboarding in the winter. In the summer, we will call this paradise their new summer camp. We will certainly take advantage of all the amenities in this special community.

After we closed, but before stepping through the door, I made it a point to bless our home in the only way I could imagine: by honoring my husband, his memory, and his legacy. In his death, he gave me life, and I am eternally grateful for that

With fragile hearts, our children spoke directly to their dad in heaven, and I thanked him for never, ever, ever leaving our sides. With arms outstretched, we held his essential being carefully, and in unison, we lowered his ashes into the water. We watched silently as the remains of the fifth blessed member of our family disappeared.

I shall call this creek "River of Peace" because it reminds me that I have a right to live with purpose and passion, a right to dream big, and a right to inner peace in the chaos of it all.

Guess what? So do you.

11.23.13

I loved seeing my children's faces today as we walked past the ski lift and reminisced about moments we spent there with John-Marlon. It was equally heartwarming to see them swim in the same pool where their father took his last swim. He literally mustered every ounce of strength to enjoy his final moments, to be able to live it up a little with his family. Some would avoid revisiting a place that brings back so many fond memories, but I have purposely made every effort to experience the old *and* to create new memories in those spaces.

Only sky separates us from being physically together. Death has lost its unbearable sting because no matter the distance, he is with us, relishing the peace we feel in our magical paradise. We are blessed to be here in his honor. I am grateful for my past, humbled by my present, and hopeful for my future.

11.24.13

If I asked you to describe the woman I just posted on my newsfeed, what would you say? Okay, I'll say it for you: hot, cute, sexy, put-together, powerful, full of life. You wouldn't say: sad, depleted, lost. Of course not! Would you believe that this picture was taken two-and-a-half years ago at one of the lowest points in my life? I always faked it.

What's my point? First, stop putting yourself last on your list. You will have more to give when there is more of you to give.

When you see all those happy pictures on Facebook, remember that there is a story behind each photo—and not all are what they portray. I am living proof. Don't compare your life to anyone else's life; you don't know what someone else may be struggling with behind a radiant smile.

11.26.13

Some believe we face war in our own lives so that we can learn to be more compassionate to others. If we didn't experience pain, would we have compassion? I don't think we would. That's not to say that we deserve pain, but life is, unfortunately, not fair. Some of us are chosen and will be chosen for such trying experiences so that we can share the lessons of our own personal journeys.

When I was single and narcissistic and traveled for sheer fun, I would dread it if a child sat behind me in a plane. If he or she dared to kick my seat, I would boil. I would turn around to give the child "that look," and the parents would get the evil eye too. More often than not, I would ask them to control their little creation.

In due time, God blessed me with a child on the autism spectrum. Boy, did I ever learn compassion for children, especially special-needs children. Now if a kid kicks my seat, I turn around and smile, and I assure the little one that it's okay to keep kicking.

11.27.13

More often than I would like to admit, we both thought our marriage was a mistake—until death knocked on our door. As death knocked harder and louder, the movie of our lives played in our heads, and we both learned quickly what compassion for one another actually meant. We were able to step out of our bodies and into each other's souls to appreciate one another on a level so extremely deep that we emerged as soul mates. Now that is true compassion, and God's work indeed.

As I flex my compassion muscle this holiday season, I realize I have much work head, and I welcome it. I will approach it with an open heart by listening more, hugging tighter, judging a lot less, and learning that in the silence of sixty seconds, I can avoid a lifetime of regret just by waiting a minute between thinking bad thoughts and saying them. My words must be overflowing with love and light.

May God grant you all health, peace in your heart, and joy that makes you giggle this holiday season. Of course, a sprinkle of compassion will not hurt either.

12.1.13

We are all just passersby on this earth, and we can only hope that when our loved ones take their last breaths, they know how much we loved them.

None of us are making it out alive, and as painful as that sounds, we have to use that vulnerable feeling to love with an open heart. We do not know what tomorrow holds. Rich, poor, famous, homeless, man, woman, child—we are all going home one day.

The inner peace I hold in my heart after my husband's death exists because I was able to say everything that was in my heart. I told him how much I loved him, watched him reach for heaven, and even held his hand as he took his final breath. I am blessed. When pain overcomes me, I keep perspective. If your loved ones are still alive, you have another opportunity to make a sequel to the movie of your life. If your loved ones have passed, keep perspective and find the light in their stories. There is light, I promise. We can live in darkness, but we will never thrive in this, the one life that we have been given. This has been a trying year for many; let us send prayers to us all, and may our angels watch over us with special attention.

11.28.13

Happy Thanksgiving. Many blessings to you! Health, inner peace, and joy!

Live in the moment; we do not know what tomorrow will bring. Try your best to live with an attitude of gratitude today and every day after. I hope you are all having a warm Thanksgiving. As for us four, we have no tears, only smiles. Your positive energy and love for us on this difficult day has been received with open arms. We are forever a family of five.

12.1.13

Today, I began decorating with my kids, but we couldn't find three-quarters of our decorations because only John-Marlon would have known where they are buried in the garage. But we managed to make lemons from lemonade. Our job was not too shabby!

The old me would have been consumed by keeping up with the everyone else's spectacular décor, but I am present enough to realize that the pressure of keeping up will be a horror show for my emotional well-being.

If stress has overcome you this holiday season, as it always did me—just stop and really think about the origins of *Christ*-mas. I don't think my kids will remember in years to come that our Christmas tree in 2013 did not win any awards, but twenty years from now, they will most likely recall the hot chocolate and the hugs I am about to bestow on them in the next five minutes.

If we're lucky, a good life is made up of many beautiful small moments, and I know this one will count. Living in the moment is a gift if we can embrace the idea—as far-reaching as it sounds. Don't let insignificant stress steal your joy because it robs your children of their joy. Keep what is dear to you close; the rest is icing on the cake. Happy holidays!

12.2.13

My inner thinking has evolved in such a short period of time that it's causing me to have an exceptionally emotional evening. When I think of the *ugly* moments of my past life, I realize I had much more outer beauty than inner. I just didn't know any better, and I have forgiven myself for the war that existed in my own head throughout my marriage. I don't readily revisit those moments, but I'm being forced to as I write these final entries of my book. The pain is greater than the day I lost my husband.

I am so tremendously sad for that young woman who had no idea how to live and love—and I want desperately to hug her. I have no regrets; it's just that returning to these painful memories is forcing me to realize how much precious time was unnecessarily wasted. I can't reverse time or the needless, ugly wrestling with myself, but in realizing this and changing or evolving, I know that a discussion of my pain will become a source of inspiration and guidance to someone else. That, in turn, is my blessing.

Please pray for my clarity and that I can tell, truthfully—as hard as it is—the most difficult parts of my life story with compassion, dignity, and respect. For a month now, I have been avoiding, yet I made a promise to myself that this is the week I will write with a full heart. It will be written.

12.3.13

In response to my post last night, I received a message in my inbox from a high school friend. She told me that I need to stop being so dramatic, and it kept going on an' on. She basically told me to stop having a pity party.

My initial response to this person is that I was grateful for the honesty, and these comments are a reminder that I must be careful with every post I write because people are looking to me for their dose of positivity. I am happy to take on that role, and I actually love it. I thank you for caring enough to reel me back into the light.

However, I own my past and embrace it. I have no regrets, and I would not change any of it. The pain I felt in my heart last night was not because I am living in my past. It comes because I have to revisit the "ugly" parts of who I used to be. I'm done with those. I am no longer that person, and the only reason I have to go there is to share with those who may be in the same frame of mind and still have the time to change.

I am diving into the muck so I can speak openly about the lessons that have made me who I am today. If I didn't feel pain about my growth, I don't think I would be human. I have transformed overnight from a lost girl to a woman with vision in a matter of days. It is joyful, but that much more painful, when growth happens so quickly. It's like I became a billionaire overnight. So friends, please continue to check me if I drive off course with my posts, but please recognize that I am writing a book and have to go places that otherwise I would not visit. I am writing honestly and digging deeply so my pain will be someone else's blessing.

John-Marlon and I made peace. We ended as soul mates, and we were able to recognize that this is the way our story was meant to be told and then to end—here on earth. We had a beautiful life and lived a hundred years of learning together. We were blessed to have found each other, and in the end, we connected in a way that was miraculous and magical.

12.5.13

Two trees in my backyard bring certain thoughts to mind this morning. I think that the separation between life and death is merely sky.

I appreciate how these two trees could coexist—one alive and one wilted away—already defeated by the inevitable winter. We are just the same. Sometimes, we are full of life, and sometimes, we are merely wilted spirits. Those two feelings can coexist in the same space because that is what makes us human.

I wake up every morning and realize that my journey is a blessing. However, at the end of the day, I wish I could have my husband back. My choice is to live in the space of gratitude and not nurture the parts that weigh me down and deplete my soul of what it desperately needs to grow. For me, that is gratitude, surrendering, and faith.

As you tackle your day and scroll through your Facebook news feed of posts on how to "fix your life," remember that they are merely personal insights shared by humans—that their "offerings" do not mean these writers have it all figured out. They too are wilted flowers one day and robust trees the next. Nurture your soul by applying one thing you read, hear, or learn from someone else who speaks to your soul. Overwhelming yourself with fifty things you want to change now will defeat your spirit. Change happens just as a flower blooms—with love and precious time.

12.7.13

Seven months, huh? Wow, babe. I blinked, and you have been gone seven months.

If I die old, will you still be young when we meet in heaven? If I honor your wishes and remarry in the far-distant future, will we still be destined to be together? These are just crazy questions that pop into my head. By the way, I don't mind being a cougar in heaven (in case you were wondering).

Today, you saw me crying hysterically in yoga; those were tears of joy because I felt that your embrace was the strongest it's been since you passed. Thank you. Please do that again soon.

Remember how I used to complain every year about the expensive gifts you gave me for the holidays? We both know I can't complain about that anymore. I am so extremely sorry for not knowing that your love language was through gifts. If I had known, I would have been more gracious in receiving them, and sneakier about returning them. :)

I wanted you to know that I bought myself a new ski outfit in your honor. The price tag on the jacket made me pretty uncomfortable, which means it's just like every other Christmas present you gave me. Guess what? I don't feel guilty. I love it, and it's going to look great on me because it's so pretty, and I deserve it! Merry Christmas to me from you!

Next year, I don't want any virtual presents. Please just give me a warm embrace like you gave me today. I love you, I miss you, and I will see you on the other side (God-willing, not for some time). I have to raise our three children, and I hope I will welcome our grandchildren to share your legacy.

I will always and forever love you. I am living with passion, just as you taught me. After seven months of grieving and celebrating your life through writing, I hope I have made you proud; actually, I know I have. You have been my guiding light throughout.

As 2013 comes to a close, I will not remember it with hate, disgust, or stamp a label on it to represent the pain the year brought me. I will remember it as the year I lost you, but I also found *the real you*. It was the year I opened my protected heart and shared with the world our journey in the hope that I could turn my pain into a blessing for someone else through the lessons we learned.

My heart tells me I succeeded because this peace in my heart cannot mean anything else. You will not be forgotten, my love. You have clearly left your mark here on this earth. I look forward to the day we find each other, eyes interlocked, and we touch—a touch well worth a lifetime of waiting.

Epilogue? (Well, Not Really.)

In the last seven months, I have exposed my soul. About 99 percent of the posts I have shared come from lessons I have learned from my past. Not sharing from a place that revolves around my husband is like divorcing him. Am I asking for permission from you (my biggest supporters) to set me free from my past? Am I admitting that I deserve to live, love again, and break free of what once was in a life that has been my security blanket, my safe haven, and pretty much my world?

I am a little sad. No, no, no. I am *a lot* sad! I have to admit that it's like I'm mourning his death for the first time. You may think I'm pretty good with words, but today I can't seem to string them together coherently. It's not that I don't ever want to write about him again, but it's time. It's time to move on and live forward. In letting John-Marlon go, I am really keeping him for my children and myself.

Although it was once hard to comprehend, my pain has transcended into a glorious blessing. I thank God every day that he has shown me tremendous mercy in being able to smile through the tears and experience joy despite the fact that a piece of my heart will forever be missing. That missing part of my heart will keep me humble—in gratitude and faith that God is in control. I just need to be an obedient passenger.

This was my year of *redemption* because I was able to make peace with my past. My past does not own or define me; it simply sets the benchmark for how I want to live the rest of my life. I can smell and taste 2014; I even know her name. I have no unrealistic expectations, but I do have faith that meeting *resurrection* will be a most amazing spiritual journey.

Epilogue

·····················

February 3, 2014

Last night, I pressed *send*. My completed manuscript was on its way to the publisher.

Of course, I must have been thrilled.

No.

I had a meltdown.

It arrived unexpectedly, and because I still had enough of a rational mind left to dictate the terms, I decided to investigate further. I immediately realized that this awful pain urged me to notice something. And what I noticed was that the epilogue I had written for my book was far from what must be told.

I am not sure what triggered my next action, but I decided to nurture the pain and listen to songs that reminded me of Marlon. By the way, he has always been Marlon to me. I had to call him John-Marlon for the sake of the book because ten years ago, he went from using his middle name to using his first name. Ah, it is so liberating to call him Marlon.

In listening to *vallenatos*, a type of beautiful Colombian folk music that Marlon loved, the floodgates opened. I cried uncontrollably, expressing the most pain I have felt since his passing. I repeated the same depressing *vallenato* and cried for a solid two hours. I only stopped pressing *play* after I came up with a brilliant notion. At the risk of sounding crazy, I will share without shame.

I stood up, wiped my tears, and stretched out my arms. I tilted my head up and smiled at the air, but the air wasn't an empty space. I imagined he was there. I interlocked arms with him and closed my eyes. I strategically placed us back in the Queens nightclub where we first fell lustfully in love in 1997. I imagined our bodies tonight were just as in sync as they were when we graced the dance floor all those fifteen years. We danced the song in its entirety, and as it came to an abrupt end, I refused to open my eyes.

Standing alone was too painful. I yearned for his love. I refused to let this moment leave me. Instead, I allowed my mind to take me from the nightclub back to his apartment, where I experienced physical and emotional exhilaration that made him my addiction. I opened my eyes to my own light laughter, remembering the good times, but I still felt the tightness in my chest.

When I decided it was time to wrap up this solo party, I popped in my meditation CD and was out for the night.

I awoke this morning to itchy and swollen eyes. As usual, before I threw off the covers and left bed, I thanked God for his mercy and asked Marlon for guidance. The heaviness in my heart could have pulled me back into bed, but once again, I welcomed the freeing experience of another good cry.

Pain and disappointment are inevitable, but what I choose to do with those will dictate the quality of my life, and my children's lives. My pain is no different from anyone else's pain, but I like to think that the pain of my permanent scar is Marlon's way of reminding me that he once lived—and that his life with our family mattered. For that reason, I will carry that pain to honor him with the understanding that the feeling can live only in a small compartment of my heart because the rest of it must be filled with the here and now—just as he taught me.

The Last Word

God chose me to manage my pain in a way that led me to write our story. God used writing as the source of my healing, but I have a powerful gut feeling—or could it be a conviction. I think Marlon's death was meant to change my life and the lives of others—perhaps even yours.

CPSIA information can be obtained at www.ICGtesting.com
Printed in the USA
BVOW01s1152100614

355952BV00001B/4/P